EDUCATION THAT IS CHRISTIAN

EDUCATION
That Is
CHRISTIAN

LOIS E. LeBAR

FLEMING H. REVELL COMPANY
OLD TAPPAN, NEW JERSEY

Printed in the United States of America

Library of Congress Cataloging in Publication Data
Le Bar, Lois Emogene, date
    Education that is Christian.

    Includes bibliographical references.
    1. Christian education. I. Title.
BV1471.2.L398   1981   268'.6   81-2339
ISBN 0-8007-1258-7   AACR2

Acknowledgment is made to the following for permission to reprint copyrighted material:

Christian Publications, Inc. and A. W. Tozer for material from A. W. Tozer's *The Pursuit of God,* copyright 1948 by Christian Publications, Inc.

Evangelical Teacher Training Association for material in Chapter III, the section headed "Method with the Samaritan Woman."

J. R. Gibb for material from *Dynamics of Participative Groups* by J. R. Gibb, Grace N. Platts, Lorraine F. Miller, published by John S. Swift Co., 1951.

National Education Association for material from Daniel L. Marsh's "The Place of Religion in Education."

PREFACE

Through the centuries educators have been advocating one theory of education after another, continually experimenting, continually rejecting old theories. They keep asking, "How can we get the results we want in our teaching?"

Three essential elements constitute a teaching situation: teacher, learner, and content. What is the role of the teacher? The role of the learner? How can we best use content? Sometimes one of these elements has been considered primary, with the others minimized. The way these elements are related to each other determines our philosophy of education. No arrangement has been accorded widespread approval and given universal recognition.

But educators who are Christian have a source for deriving educational principles that endure, that transcend historical fluctuations. They have a Book of God-given revelation that is impervious to the passage of time. No, the Bible is not a handbook of methods, but because it contains so many specifics, we can derive principles from its doctrines and events. Everything that is done is done in some manner. We can study that manner. From the whole of Scripture we can discern HOW the Lord works and HOW we can work with Him. We can discover the divine principles inherent in the structure of the universe.

Of course variations in knowledge and cultures make a difference, but in implementation rather than in principle. The acceleration of science and technology has resulted in new specific needs, amazing possibilities in communication and visualization, and complex equipment. Yet the essen-

tial nature of man, his inner operations, and God's requirements do not change. Though a classroom in our day may
look very different from one of another era, the basic in-
teractions of teacher, learner, and content may be the
same.

The purpose of this book is to explore God's ways of
teaching mankind, so that we need not waste time and
energy—so that our efforts may be raised to the level of
LIFE, fulness of life, in cooperation with the Lord of life.
No other system has for its center the Personality who is the
Center of the universe. No other system has the Maker of
heaven and earth as its Author, Teacher, and Content. No
other system has an invisible Teacher who can work within
a learner as well as upon him. No other has divine content
that never needs to be revised.

Christian teaching should have a plus quality that is superior to all other teaching. It is distinctive, of its own kind,
with its own methods and results. Its standards are admit-
tedly very high, but commensurate results are promised.

What role can the human teacher play without usurping
the ministry of the divine Teacher or denying learners their
legitimate activity? How can the learner assimilate the content so that it becomes his very life? How can the content
be used as the means of developing full-orbed life without
becoming sterile verbalism? In other words, how can the
Master Teacher work in His own way through us?

In this discussion various versions of the Bible have been
used. Sometimes a very free rendering of the Scriptural
emphasis seems to bring its implications closer home to
teachers today. Through His Word the Lord wants to speak
a personal word to us today in relation to our own Christian
teaching.

CONTENTS

EDUCATION THAT IS CHRISTIAN

I

NEED OF FOUNDATIONS FOR CHRISTIAN TEACHING

What is the nature of education that is truly Christian? In the words of Daniel L. Marsh:

Education should make us live life with zest, with gusto, with exuberance. But so much that passes for education takes away the wonder of life, and puts us in deadly peril of things named and classified. So much that passes for education is only the smoke of a futile fire that has done nothing but consume life. The reason is because so much that passes for education lacks the most important element.

Materialism makes for sensationalism, for jazz, for the "fed-up" attitude. It makes life stale and flat and unprofitable. But the right kind of education, education that holds to the spiritual conception and that has room for God in it, calls us from apathies that benumb and deaden the soul.

Thus religion is the vital element in full-orbed education. It pioneers for education. It adds a sense of responsibility to academic freedom. It breathes a spirit of reverence into the quest of truth. It establishes a center of moral authority in the individual's life. It gives a sense of values. It glorifies humdrum drudgeries. It brings fulfillment to life with dynamic peace!

Get all the education you can. Master as much of the intensive and extensive fields of knowledge as possible, but with all your getting, get wisdom. Remember always that the fear of the Lord is the beginning of wisdom.

Know history, and experience the history of redemption.

Study geography, and learn the way to the River of Life and the City whose Builder and Maker is God.

Study geology, and plant your feet upon the Rock of Ages.

Study zoology, and bow in reverence before the majesty of the Lion of the tribe of Judah.

Study biology, and begin now the Life Eternal.

Study botany, and yield your soul to the sweet influence of its Rose of Sharon and Lily of the Valley.

Study astronomy, and follow the gleam of your soul's Bright and Morning Star that has risen with healing in His beams.

Study psychology, and sit at the feet of Him who knew what was in man.

Study law, and light your torch in the flame that burned on Mount Sinai.

Study medicine and keep *en rapport* with the Great Physician.

Study business administration, and be fervent in spirit, serving the Lord.

Study art, and practice the art of fine living.

Study philosophy, and remember always that the highest philosophy is the formula of a perfect life.[1]

"Education should make us live life with zest, with gusto, with exuberance." Does the teaching of our evangelical Bible schools emanate zest, gusto, exuberance? Does our evangelical teaching throb and pulsate with life? Is the Lord Jesus Christ, who Himself is Life, the only source of life, so near and so real in our teaching that lives are changed each week? Is teaching considered a great adventure with the Master Teacher? Are our most promising young people challenged to make teaching a fine art because they've experienced the excitement of working with the Lord Himself?

Christian teaching operates at the level of life. Anything less is sub-Christian. The Christian life, fulness of life, the abundant life, embraces the whole man and has implications for the whole of life here and now as well as for eternity.

How do our young people leave their Sunday school classrooms on Sunday morning? With eyes sparkling with new vision and insight? With serious determination to practice the will of God? With chin up ready to face an unbelieving world in the power of the Spirit? With deep questions about God Himself? Too often they are glad for release from a dull, boring session.

ROUTINE INSTEAD OF LIFE

Instead of vibrating with life, too often the Bible school session goes more like this:

You, the teacher, come to Sunday school with your lesson well prepared. You've really studied it. You think you could talk much longer than the allotted forty-five minutes on this lesson. It's about Christ healing, and the application is good too. You hope the class will sit still and listen carefully, because you'll never be able to say all you have to say unless they do.

The pupils arrive and are they ever "wound up"! One of their school friends has been in an auto accident the night before and is in the hospital. A boy who saw the accident has to tell everyone all about it. You begin the lesson, but they don't pay attention— they continue to whisper. Finally you tell them they must be quiet. They stop talking, but you have a feeling that they aren't really listening. The wonderful application is made, but seems to have little effect. You ask for discussion. No one has a word to say, while just a minute ago you had quite a time getting them to quiet down.

You leave Sunday school feeling defeated. What was wrong?

You said every word you'd planned to say. If they'd only listened!
(Zoe Bason)

The following is the report of a young man's visit to a
Senior Sunday school class:

The attitude of the teachers was one of the strongest impressions that I had about this Sunday school. They displayed genuine devotion for the Lord and for their classes. The teacher I observed just beamed forth his love. There was also great emphasis on the Word of God.

But the Bible was taught from a heavenly, far-off viewpoint that made it lose much of its earthly, daily value. Tradition seemed to have such a strong hold on the school that the leaders' eyes seemed to be closed to the immediate needs of a group of young people who were desperately hungry for spiritual reality. One of the fellows promptly informed me that he came because it was what was expected of him. There was no expectant attitude, no opportunity for expression, no rapport between teacher and pupils. The prevailing philosophy seemed to be that teachers need only to speak the words of eternal life. No guidance or application of the truth was given in any phase of the youth program.

The young people had a degree of intellectual knowledge but little practical experience as a result of it. They knew how prayers should sound and for whom they should pray, so they spoke the words, without evidence of true communion with God. The printed materials that the school used were good, but were used as an end in themselves rather than as a means to the end of spiritual life and growth. The leaders tried hard, but grew discouraged because they saw little results.

Honestly my heart ached for that Sunday school. Here were teachers with a burden for their classes, yet they were only failing them. No one had shown them the Scriptural way of working. They had God's glorious good news without understanding how to communicate it to others. (Paul Robert Palmer)

Routine always has a deadening effect, even Bible routine. It is no more natural for us human beings to do God's work in God's way than it is for us to discover God's way of salvation for ourselves. His ways are higher and better than our ways. And some kind of method is always involved in action; we can't say we aren't interested in method. For if we don't work in God's way, we work in our own natural way. If the Spirit isn't in control, the self life dominates. Our old self life is always clamoring to intrude into spiritual activities.

In a searching little book, *The Pursuit of God,* A. W. Tozer of the Christian and Missionary Alliance analyzes the current situation very sharply:

There is today no lack of Bible teachers to set forth correctly the principles of the doctrines of Christ, but too many of these seem satisfied to teach the fundamentals of the faith year after year, strangely unaware that there is in their ministry no manifest Presence, nor anything unusual in their personal lives. They minister constantly to believers who feel within their breasts a longing which their teaching simply does not satisfy.[2]

Sound Bible exposition is an imperative *must* in the Church of the Living God. Without it no church can be a New Testament church in any strict meaning of that term. But exposition may be carried on in such way as to leave the hearers devoid of any true spiritual nourishment whatever. For it is not mere words that nourish the soul, but God Himself, and unless and until the hearers find God in personal experience they are not the better for having heard the truth. The Bible is not an end in itself, but a means to bring men to an intimate and satisfying knowledge of God, that they may enter into Him, that they may delight in His Presence, may taste and know the inner sweetness of the very God Himself in the core and center of their hearts.[3]

This same lack of spiritual reality and power commensurate with evangelical doctrine is noted by other leaders such as Vance Havner, who writes articles with the captions, "Are You a Firsthander?" and "Is Your Christian Experience Original?" He says:

Many believers never press through to a firsthand experience of the deeper Christian life. We live on the hand-me-down teaching and experience of saints and scholars of other ages. We live on the sayings and doings of popular preachers and leaders but it is canned goods. We do not grow our own gardens.[4]

In one of the soundest, most powerful pulpits of our land a dedicated man of God was pouring out his heart to his congregation one Sunday morning. He pleaded with his people to live the Christ life, the deeper life, the Spirit-filled life. Downstairs in the church building at that very moment a young man was leading Junior Church. He was asking normal, lively young Juniors to sing one adult song after another with little meaning, for no thought was given to the words. He was merely concerned that the singing sound good. Occasionally he had to stop to scold a youngster for inattention to the singing. For the last song he said, "Come on now, sing this one loud." The selection turned out to be "My Jesus, I love Thee, I know Thou art mine." Those Juniors did sing it loud and lustily, trying to outdo and entertain each other.

This same stereotyped routine rather than dynamic life characterized that church's Sunday school as well as its Junior Church. The young members of that Christian community were growing up with "a form of godliness denying the power thereof" from their earliest, most formative years. The very evils that the beloved pastor was bewailing were inherent in the training of the children of his church!

Nothing will take the place of sound doctrine and the facts of the Word of God. But it is possible to starve people with Biblical facts, to make doctrine a substitute for spiritual reality, to fail our people by denying them the intimate personal experience with the Lord Himself who alone will satisfy the deepest longings of the human heart.

We expend great energy and expense to enlist, prepare,

and send missionaries to the far corners of the earth with the gospel, and so we should, many more of them. They must be prepared to serve in a foreign culture with a foreign language. Why don't we have enough missionary recruits to evangelize the world? Why don't we have money enough to send those who want to go? We are failing to reach the heathen at our doorstep who could be won with our own language in our own culture with a fraction of the effort. Thousands who have been *exposed* to the truth in our Sunday schools have never been *enlisted* for Christ. They have been part of the crowd that thronged Christ but have never touched the hem of His garment for themselves (Mark 5:24–34).

USE OF MAN-MADE EDUCATIONAL SYSTEMS

A chief reason for the lack of life and power and reality in our evangelical teaching is that we have been content to borrow man-made systems of education instead of discovering God's system. Secular educators do not give central place to the unique revelation of God's Word that is communicated by God's Spirit. Our distinctive content calls for distinctive treatment.

A group of graduate students made a survey of the total program of an evangelical church that had been a leader in teacher training for its area. Because most of the teachers in this church held certificates earned by taking six teacher training courses, the students expected them to be superior teachers. They were surprised to find that the teacher training had made very little difference in the actual teaching ministry of the church, and they searched for the reasons.

Observation of each agency and activity of the church revealed the fact that the teachers had read manuals, had discussed their contents, had answered questions on the content that were factual, general, and abstract. They ei-

ther did not see the relation of the principles they had
studied to their own classroom teaching or they did not
know how to translate the principles into procedures. The
manuals had taught and practiced Herbartian philosophy
with its systematic methodology of content, relying upon
association psychology and automatic transfer of knowing
into feeling and willing and doing. This philosophy had not
satisfactorily functioned since the teachers experienced
very little change as a result of finishing the courses.

Why should Christians borrow a system of education
from the secular world? Why should we not derive from
God's revelation our own philosophy, God's own ways of
working that are inherent in the very structure of the universe? Of course there will be correlation between the secular and the spiritual, for both deal with the same human
learner. Secular educators have studied the learner much
more thoroughly than have Christians. But the foundations
and the orientation of Christian education are distinctive if
they are truly Christian. Every area of life that the Word of
God enters is changed.

Because some of our evangelicals have not bothered to
search God's Word for their philosophy, they lack the unity
of purpose and method that should strengthen their cause.
At the same Sunday school convention in the same building
it is not uncommon to find two workshop leaders who both
seek the leading of the Spirit, yet are poles apart in their
suggestions as to actual teaching methods. In an era when
many evangelical groups are producing their own literature
and visual aids, the underlying philosophy of these materials differs widely because each leader does that which is
right in his own eyes. As all of us grow in our comprehen-
sion of the truth and grow nearer to Him who is the Truth
as well as the Life, we shall come nearer to each other.
Then we can do more to strengthen each other's hands
instead of competing with each other.

TEACHING THAT IS ONLY POOR LAY PREACHING

In a day when the preaching ministry of the church is producing results, the teaching ministry is lagging far behind. In Scripture these two ministries are not the same, as we sometimes assume them to be. Two distinct words are used. Christ Jesus came preaching, for He first proclaimed to any who would hear that the Kingdom of God was at hand. Then when He had chosen His disciples and when He was sought by people who had witnessed His authoritative preaching and His signs, He spent most of His time teaching. He is more often called Teacher than Preacher.

What is the distinction between preaching and teaching? Is there any reason why teaching shouldn't be just as inspirational as preaching? We preach and teach to both saved and unsaved. Why is it that pupils are usually divided into small groups for teaching? Teaching is causing to learn, a term usually used with an indirect object, "teaching the people." Preaching is heralding the good news, used with the direct object, "preaching the word." Not that the Lord didn't teach people *content,* or that He didn't preach *to people.* But the emphasis is different in each case. The peculiar genius of teaching is the small intimate group in which overt interaction is possible.

We need both preaching and teaching, each with its own methods. Pastors are called and trained to preach. Teachers should be called and trained to teach. It is amazing that a pastor will allow lay teachers with no training to preach at his congregation in Sunday school the hour before he has a chance at them. By that time they are ready to run around the block, not to sit through another sermon.

Many an adult who grew up in church confesses with regret that his patience has been so sorely tried by being expected to sit through so much talking that now, even though he wants to listen, his mind automatically turns off whenever a person starts. We train our church people to be professional listeners rather than leaders. The Scriptures declare that teaching is more than talking, though it sometimes is talking.

LACK OF MATURE EVANGELICAL LEADERSHIP

In this critical day in which we live, Christian leaders are needed in every walk of life. The church of Christ should be developing these leaders by a program of training from birth to death. Every believer has been given a gift of the Holy Spirit for the building of the body of Christ. Our talent or ability is God's gift to us; the skillful use of that ability is our gift to Him. We'll never know the thrill of fulfilling the purpose for which we were born until we have developed our gift. We'll never know fulness of life until we're in the center of God's will, making our unique contribution to the church of the living God.

If the potentialities of all Christians were being developed from the earliest years, the adults in our churches would be producing—producing Christian life, witness, literature, art, music, and skill in all the vocations that are worthy of a follower of the Son of God. Each church would be a miniature Bible institute, a laboratory for discovering and implementing eternal truth. Each church would be alive with study and projects and expansion programs.

Then when leaders are needed to lead discussion groups and demonstrate Scriptural methods at conventions, our laymen would be ready to make their contribution. When editors look for young people to train as writers and artists, they'd be able to find good prospects. When we look for Sunday school departments that are doing a bang-up piece of work for others to visit, we'd have some in each geographical area.

In an editorial in *Eternity* magazine, Donald Grey Barnhouse analyzes the difference between the British Keswick convention and a similar meeting in the United States. He says:

Beyond question there are spiritual depths in England which are not known here. The British leaders who have visited America confess that they find a lightness, a lack of spiritual depth, which disconcerts them. On the other hand, I have talked with American leaders who have been in Britain who find there what we would call a woeful lack of biblical knowledge.[5]

Why should not Biblical knowledge and spiritual depth go together? How are we going to justify before the Lord a lack of either?

II

OUTSTANDING PATTERNS
OF EDUCATION

Why is it that some classes are vibrant with life and growth while others bog down in a morass of listlessness? Or it may even be that the class members spark their own excitement in opposition to the teacher. Where can we begin our attack on the problems of education? Since education has always been a universal problem, educators through the centuries have proposed a wide range of reforms. The various systems can be most clearly compared and contrasted by noting their emphasis on factors inside the learner and factors outside the learner.

Factors inside the learner refer to the way he feels about the whole situation. Because of his past experience with this class or other classes, was he eager to come to class today or did he have to be pressured under protest? Does he enter heartily into group work, is he indifferent toward the group, or does he bestir himself to invent his own interests? How does this class fit in with his own ambitions and values? Are his personal psychological needs for security, affection, recognition, new experiences, freedom from guilt, being met by the class? What is his attitude toward the teacher, the class members, the room and equipment? Is he physically comfortable and in good health?

In the free play period of a nursery or kindergarten we find these inner factors dominant. Here the children themselves decide to which of the interest centers they will go, how long they will stay there, what they will do with the materials, whether they will play alone or with other children. Here they freely express their feelings toward materials and people, they learn what they want to learn, they experience success or failure according to their own evaluation of themselves. Though they are continually interacting with outer factors in the environment, they themselves determine what goes on. The activities may be educative or not, depending upon the direction of their own choices and the supervision they receive from outside themselves. Teachers are usually ready to step in with outside guidance when the children need it.

Factors outside the learner are mainly the teacher, the course of study, the class members, and the room. Of course the place of the teacher himself is strategic. Does he consider his role to be that of benevolent dictator, or the most experienced member of the group? He may rule in the sense that everything that happens depends upon what he wants, how he wants it, and when he wants it. Or he may include the group in the planning and executing and evaluating. He determines whether the methods shall revolve around himself and his oral and book presentation, whether models and specimens and other visual aids shall be brought into the classroom, whether the learners shall interact with each other in the process of learning or whether they shall talk only to him. He may not have complete control over the physical environment, but he can usually regulate the temperature, lighting, arrangement of furniture. The course of study may be strictly definitive or it may suggest only a broad area of interest. The class members may be free to contribute a great deal to each other or they may have a competitive spirit toward each other.

It is easier to manipulate outer factors than inner factors because the teacher can sit in his office and decide exactly what is going to happen in the classroom—or at least what he hopes will happen. He tries to deal with only one of the types of factors involved. If he allows the pupils to become actively involved, anything could happen. He may not feel adequate to cope with inner factors if he brought them into play, so he may feel more secure if he concentrates on the outer that he can control. The simplest method is for the teacher to organize the course of study logically, hand it out piecemeal to the students, and ask them to give it back in the same form. Moreover, if his aim is merely to teach content, he may feel no need of bothering with inner factors.

But what happens to many a teaching situation in which the attitudes of the pupils are not considered? How does the teacher know that they are going to sit still and study the content and give it back? What often happens inside pupils when they are asked to study and to reproduce knowledge content? When inner factors revolt against the outer process, what does that do to the teacher? On the other hand, what happens when inner factors are given full rein without adequate guidance? What then seems to be the central problem in education?

EMPHASIS ON OUTER FACTORS

A quick survey of the history of education shows that the prevailing tendency of human nature is to overemphasize outer factors. In the ancient nations of Assyria-Babylonia,

Egypt, India, and China, outer elements were practically the only consideration. The general outlook was backward rather than forward, the major aim being to preserve the past or the status quo rather than to improve them. Memory and imitation stand out as the chief methods in a transmissive, authoritarian system. Because study was not interesting, discipline was severe. Because individuality was suppressed, art and science were undeveloped, literature barren and formulistic. Religion was polytheistic and impersonal. Because religion made no appeal to inner light and will, morality was superficial, ethics divorced from conduct. The sacred texts were usually traditions passed on by memory with little attention to meaning and application. Even when education gave priests or artisans practical preparation for taking their places in society, this preparation was mechanical and stereotyped. The stress was upon outward conformity.

The education that the Lord God gave the Jewish people whom He chose for His own purposes was theocentric and practical, with a salutary balance between inner and outer factors. They were to glorify Him in national destiny and personal character. He taught them by precept and example, by knowing and doing, by questions and moral discipline, memorization and sensory appeal. Their worship of Him and their daily morality were closely connected. These were also the methods of Christ Jesus, the Master Teacher, which will be discussed at length in the next chapter.

Apostolic education was also dynamic and individual. The Word of God was studied and practiced by the illumination and power of the Holy Spirit. Knowing, feeling, and doing were balanced in doctrine, worship, and holy living. Believers multiplied themselves by assembling together, building themselves up in the faith, and witnessing wherever they were. The New Testament set the pattern for a holy, powerful church through the ages.

But soon early church instruction degenerated into formal lectures and catechetical questions and answers. Theology was developed to relate Christian doctrine to pagan philosophy or to show its contrast, church authority and organization were developed to stabilize the church. These trends led directly to the ascetic and ecclesiastical formalism of the Middle Ages. As in the ancient nations, methods again grew transmissive, repressive, and stereotyped. The invading barbarians were converted outwardly through mechanical profession of faith and ceremony.

The Renaissance period saw the revival of an inquiring spirit and a widened horizon for learning. At its height the schoolmen felt that they had brought faith and reason into complete accord as they systematized the doctrine that is still the basis of the Roman church. But the thinking in this age declined into aimless controversy and ended as authoritarianism that neither extended nor applied knowledge.

Church abuses and the scientific spirit of the Renaissance led to the Reformation with its return to the authority of the Scriptures, personal salvation, and judgment. Again outer and inner factors were balanced for a short time, with concentration upon reading of the Bible in the vernacular, responsibility of parents for child training in the home, the relating of knowledge to virtue, and of faith to civic leadership.

But at the close of the Reformation the quicker method of preaching began to replace the slower method of teaching, rote memorization of the catechism replaced personal study of the Scriptures. In colonial America the aim of education was holy living and dying, with religion the core of the school curriculum. Yet children were considered miniature adults, teachers heard recitations, tested memorization, and kept order with severity in a formal, repressive atmosphere.

From the inception of the Sunday school in the latter part of the eighteenth century, the aim of Christian education has usually been stated as knowledge of the Bible and conversion. Conversion has been conceived as a natural by-product of knowledge of the Bible. Most Bible teachers have labored under the impression that if they taught the outer facts of the Bible, the Holy Spirit would do the inner work of regenerating the pupil. They didn't consider it necessary for them to study human nature or to know the developmental stages through which the pupil passed.

At first pupils studied the catechism, then came the period when they were urged to memorize quantities of Scripture. At Sunday school concerts they repeated by rote what they had learned, in order to receive prizes. Finally in the nineteenth century leaders began to pay some attention to the selection of Scripture portions, the writing of lessons, grading of pupils, training of teachers, building of churches for teaching, and organization of Sunday schools. Even in the great Bible study period of 1860–1880 pupils studied the Bible factually with little understanding, little appreciation, and little relationship to daily life and problems.

Thus we see that throughout the ages teachers have most often considered their task to be that of exposing pupils to factual content and of getting them to give back in words this outer knowledge. They have relied almost wholly upon verbal communication of facts.

How much of the factual knowledge to which *you* were exposed in high school is now your personal possession? Why? Which parts of your high-school background mean most to you now? Why? Which mean least to you now? How could that material have been made operative in your life then? Can you suggest ways in which your high-school training could have been made more profitable to you?

Have you "learned" all the facts to which you've been exposed in church and Sunday school? Are you now practicing all the Scriptural truth that you "know"? Are your pupils practicing all the truth that they "know"? Why is it that we so often hear the lament, "He knows better than that; why does he do it?" How helpful is it for teachers to speak Bible facts into the air?

JOHANN FRIEDRICH HERBART (1776–1841)

In the twentieth century when Christian education sought to improve its teaching of the Bible, no one had formulated from Scripture a distinctive Christian philosophy. So few people were giving serious thought to the problems of the Bible school that no one had anything to offer from a Scriptural viewpoint. For nineteen hundred years since Christ had come to earth to bring God's great good news, no group of evangelicals had come together to establish a philosophy of Christian education. Therefore when a system was needed to offset the haphazard use of Bible texts and Bible memorization, the leaders cast about and found the system that was then enjoying great favor in the secular world; the Herbartian method.

Herbart was an intellectual who spent most of his life teaching philosophy and education at two German universities. He elevated teaching by making a real science out of it, by advocating formal steps based upon a carefully thought-through psychology. Because he set forth a logical system of teaching content and held the high aims of personal character and social morality, his system was transferred to the teaching of the Bible.

Herbart considered content all-important because he thought that by relating ideas he could actually formulate the mind from without. In order to impart this knowledge, the teacher had to awaken old ideas, for the learner was interested in the ideas that he already had had. This connecting of new ideas with old is one of Herbart's greatest contributions to education, the principle of apperception as it is called. The following five formal steps of the recitation are the best-known form of Herbart's system as adapted by his followers:

1. Preparation. Past ideas related to the new idea are recalled. Only if the apperceptive masses are brought into consciousness will the pupil be interested in the new and give attention to it. If an idea cannot be brought to mind, it may be necessary to start with a familiar object and derive ideas from the sense perceptions that are obtained from it.

2. Presentation. The teacher makes the new material clear in the form of an idea or an object.

3. Association. Likenesses and differences between the old and new material are pointed out by the teacher.

4. Generalization. Concrete ideas are now raised to the level of abstraction, for this is the mind working at its highest capacity.

5. Application. The student now uses the new generalization to solve related questions in that area of knowledge, such as solving of problems in geometry or the translating of sentences of a foreign language.

By this systematic procedure the student was to receive clear new ideas that he could use. This process built up many new ideas and therefore interest on which to build other new ideas. Interest at the end of a lesson was greater than at the beginning. The mind was actually being structured from without, thought Herbart.

For Herbart the main skill in teaching was then the connecting of new ideas with old. In this task, association psychology came to the aid of the teacher, for ideas once in the mind keep seeking to return, he said. Similar ideas tend to reenforce each other until they build up strength enough to return to consciousness. Dissimilar ideas tend to repel each other. Interest is the result of the combining of associated ideas. Association psychology has now been discredited, since most of the ideas in our minds seek to escape us, not to return.

"How were Herbart's new intellectual ideas going to produce his aim of moral character?" we may ask. He explained this process by means of a "circle of thought." Since knowing is the primary function of the mind, feeling and willing and doing are automatically, inevitably derived from knowing. When ideas reenforce each other in their struggle to push back into consciousness, the result is pleasure; when they are so different that they repel each other, the result is displeasure. The totality of ideas constitutes the will that expresses itself in action. Ideas that command full attention result in action. Therefore by manipulating the pupil's ideas, the teacher is able to determine how he will feel and choose and act.

So clear, right ideas *ought* to result in moral character. If only character formation were that easy, that simple! But is it? If all of us automatically acted on the right ideas that we have, what kind of place would this world be? Of course we need to know the right ideas, but does knowing guarantee doing? Is knowledge virtue? Moreover, Herbart's concern was secular education; he was not thinking in a Christian framework.

Much of today's Bible teaching is still based on Herbartian method. The most common approach—if there is any approach—is the question, "What did we have last Sunday?" How eager does that make pupils to study the Word of God? Why isn't there usually response to that question? Because last Sunday's lesson began like that too. While the teacher presents, associates, generalizes, and even applies the new material, the pupils' minds wander off to places of their own choosing where they can actively pursue their own interests.

What does the Bible say about knowing and feeling and willing and doing? If Herbart were correct, the first and great commandment would read, "Thou shalt know" rather than "Thou shalt love." Knowing is essential, there is no question about that; but knowing does not always result in loving and doing, whereas loving is based upon knowing and is much more likely to result in doing.

O earth, earth, earth, hear the word of the Lord (Jeremiah 22:29).

O Lord, I know that the way of man is not in himself: it is not in man that walketh to direct his steps (Jeremiah 10:23).

The fear of the Lord is the beginning of wisdom: a good understanding have all they that do his commandments . . . (Psalms 111:10).

Therefore to him that knoweth to do good, and doeth it not, to him it is sin (James 4:17).

. . . what I would, that do I not; but what I hate, that do I . . . to will is present with me; but how to perform that which is good I find not. For the good that I would I do not: but the evil which I would not, that I do (Romans 7:15, 18, 19).

Knowing is neither the beginning nor the end of the transformation of character. Knowledge is not virtue, but rather the wise use of knowledge is virtue. We Christians need more than Herbartian philosophy if we are going to lead men step by step to ". . . the measure of the stature of the fulness of Christ" (Ephesians 4:13).

EMPHASIS ON INNER FACTORS

Throughout the history of education the powers and purposes of the learner himself have received much less attention than has the content to be learned. In comparatively few instances have teachers tried to guide the pupil's progress by studying his physical development, his capacities, needs, interests, and inclinations.

Early Greek education in Athens is an outstanding example of personal development. The Greeks aimed at the harmonious development of the whole person. They tried to guide the youth's natural activity into artistic and useful forms, gradually to induct him into the actual life of the community. It was not primarily an intellectual or theoretical process, but rather a moral process. The Athenian youth had a pedagogue to supervise personally his every move, his conduct, his manners, his morals. Good habits were constantly practiced so that character could be established. The child was given constant opportunity to express and control his emotions, exercise his curiosity, create something beautiful and good. A very simple curriculum was imposed on him from without: usually reading, writing, literature, religion, citizenship, music, and gymnastics. Comparatively little of his day was spent on "book work."

The most extreme position ever proposed by an advocate of man's inherent possibilities was that of Jean Jacques Rousseau (1712–1778). "Man is born free, yet is everywhere in chains!" rang out the indignation of a vagabond with the conviction of a martyr. "All is good as it comes from the hands of the Creator; all degenerates in the hands of men."

Rousseau made childhood in its own right the center of education. "Educational writers devote themselves to what a man ought to know," he protested, "without asking what a child is capable of learning. It is a mistake to try to turn his attention to matters that do not concern him in the least, such as his future interest, his happiness when he is grown." Childhood no longer becomes inferior adulthood. The stages of child nature must be studied and understood.

Rousseau's aim was to bring about changes in men rather than the acquisition of a superficial form of knowledge. His boy Émile would be large-minded not through knowledge but through the power of acquiring it. Nothing would be done for the child that he could do himself.

Rousseau probed deeply into the very heart of the teaching process when he proclaimed that curiosity and usefulness should furnish the driving power for learning. If desire to learn is aroused in a pupil, any of many methods will serve. Guidance is to be by nature and natural interests. Morality and discipline are learned by experiencing the natural consequences of behavior.

From Rousseau, Pestalozzi (1746–1827) received his seminal ideas that made over the elementary school. Pestalozzi rejected the teaching of mere words and facts in favor of drawing out the pupil's intellectual and moral powers. Sense impression gained from real objects was the basis of all instruction. His education was "a natural, symmetrical, and harmonious development of all the faculties of the child," a definition similar to that of the Greeks. He held that the child is a natural organism that unfolds its inner life according to orderly laws that teachers must discover and work with. He made many observations of the growth of children.

Friedrich Froebel (1782–1852) made more observation and accumulation of facts concerning children's natural activities. He concluded that education includes both individual and racial evolution, the process by which man fully develops his powers in relation to nature and society. Education for Froebel was the directing of the pupil's self-activity, not the imposing of content on him from outside. It was bringing ever more *out* of man rather than putting more and more *into* him. Born with all the potentialities of the race, the child was bursting to express the life and energy of his nature. He was not to be introduced to a new subject until he felt an inner need for it. On these foundations Froebel founded the kindergarten with its play, self-expression, rhythm, constructive activity, and social cooperation.

JOHN DEWEY (1859–1952)

America's leading philosopher and educator was also an exponent of concentration on the pupil's experience. At an early age Dewey professed to accept the religious teachings in which he was brought up and joined the church. But his belief was never vital enough to meet his emotional need. Later he found in the philosophy of Hegel that combined challenge to head and heart that he had missed earlier. If only his parents and his church school teachers had helped him to experience personal dealings with the Lord of life before he became one of the greatest foes of Christianity!

Today we teachers don't know which children in our churches and on our streets may be the most influential leaders of tomorrow. We may even have them in our Sunday school classes. Are we sure that their whole beings are being challenged for the Lord?

Dewey's early school life was a bore to him. The things that really mattered happened outside the schoolroom. Therefore he sought to bring real living and thinking into the classroom, to open school windows to let a breath of fresh air blow through the stuffy halls, to make school a miniature society in which people could deal with their real problems.

Dewey reacted against Herbart's theory of interest, which was stronger at the end of a lesson than at the beginning, and which was prompted by knowledge that had already been learned. Dewey held that learning was essentially problem solving, the continuous reconstruction of experience. School should provide the child opportunity for normal activity, in the course of which he meets a problem, which provides a learning situation because it causes him to think. He should clearly define the problem, collect data that bear upon the problem, and experiment with various solutions that he thinks might work. Thus he is coping with real difficulties in life situations.

Education to Dewey was life, not preparation for life. Only by living fully today is the pupil prepared to take the next step tomorrow. In the process of using materials and ideas, the child comes to understand them. He does not need to have insight into them before he can use them. He learns by doing, which involves more of himself than his mind, for activity is basic to human nature. This activity is not random flitting from one interest to another or dictated busywork, but intelligent investigation directed toward a purpose that has meaning for the learner. Very young a child begins to use the spirit of the scientific method.

Thus Dewey kept the focus of education on the pupil's own experience. Of course the pupil often feels the need of going to books or history or past experience or other people's data in order to solve his problem, but knowledge is a means to the end of achieving his own goals. He continually needs to exercise judgment and intelligence for practical purposes. The organization of the school is on the basis of experience rather than content set out to be learned.

If the school as a miniature society provides a healthy social atmosphere and environment, teachers can guide pupils in mutually helpful living and social cooperation rather than competition. In a shared enterprise in which all the group are personally involved, the rules are in the game. The teacher need not act as an outsider to enforce order, but as a most respected member of the "in-group" to share responsibility and insight with the others. Whereas the old school trained its pupils in the more passive virtues of obedience and conformity, Dewey's school sought to develop initiative and responsibility.

Underlying Dewey's whole system was the philosophy of humanistic naturalism that trusted in man and his intelligence. There is no supernature, there are no absolutes. Dewey believed that institutional religion is the greatest enemy of civilization. God should be deleted from human thinking. If the term God must be retained, it should be used to designate the active relation between the real and the ideal.

Does the pupil's experience have a place, a significant place, in a Christian framework? Are inner factors necessary in teaching? The regeneration experience takes place in the inner life of the individual. The aim of Christian education is best expressed in the words of Ephesians 4:13, "Till we all come in the unity of the faith, and of the knowledge of the Son of God, unto a perfect man, unto the

measure of the stature of the fulness of Christ." Christlikeness is an inner experience that manifests itself outwardly.

. . . we glory in tribulations also: knowing that tribulation
worketh patience; And patience, experience; and experience, hope: And hope maketh not ashamed . . . (Romans
5:3–5).

For every one that partaketh of milk is without experience of the word of righteousness; for he is a baby. But
solid food is for fullgrown men, even those who by reason
of use have their senses exercised to discern good and evil
(Hebrews 5:13,14 ASV).

. . . Whoever knows God by experience listens to us;
whoever is not a child of God does not listen to us. This is
the way to distinguish a true spiritual utterance from one
that is false. Dearly beloved, let us practice loving one
another, because love originates with God, and everyone
who practices loving is a child of God and knows God by
experience. Whoever does not love has never come to
know God by experience, because God is love (1 John 4:
6–8 WILLIAMS).

JOHN AMOS COMENIUS (1592–1670)

John Amos Comenius was a Christian who is often called
the first modern educator though he lived way back in the
seventeenth century. Because he received light both from
God's written revelation and from His second book of nature, he was able to see educational truth far in advance of
his time. Though his theology may not always have been
consistent because he was writing without the advantage of
the systematic study that has been done since his day, he
maintained a wholehearted faith directed to the glory of
God. His educational writings contain many references to
Scripture and doctrine.

At an early age his father, mother, and two sisters died,
foreboding perhaps the suffering and deprivation that at-

tended him all his life. It wasn't until he was sixteen years old that he entered a Latin secondary school, which taught the language of scholarship.

By that time he was older than the other boys, old enough to sense the dreadful abuses of the system of his day. Schools were places of torture, which he termed "slaughterhouses of the mind." Their weaknesses were due to the inefficiency of the teachers rather than to the idleness of the pupils. Discipline had to be severe because there was no grading, no interest, almost no meaning. When Comenius realized how the keen energies of youth were being dulled and wasted, he was motivated to reform measures, for he had great faith in education to raise the level of the common people.

After studying at two universities, he returned to Moravia at the age of twenty-two. Since a young man could not be ordained for the ministry until he was twenty-four, he accepted a position as director of an elementary and secondary school. Here he began to construct an easier method for learning Latin. Two years later when he was ordained, he took a pastorate where he was also inspector of a school. He then married and enjoyed two of his happiest years.

In 1621 when the Protestant persecution of the Thirty Years' War broke out and his town was plundered and burned, he lost everything he owned including his books and manuscripts. The next year his wife and two children perished in an epidemic that raged through Moravia. For the rest of his life he was in exile. But he ever dreamed of coming home and he continued steadfastly to do what he could to improve educational method. Ever strong also was his theological interest and his concern for his suffering brethren. He was later made bishop of his church.

In 1628 when all evangelicals had to leave Moravia, Comenius went to Lissa, Poland, where he had opportunity to develop his educational theories and put them into practice as director of a secondary school. He felt that if children learned their lessons quicker and easier, the time saved could be utilized to give a thorough grounding in morality and religion.

His graded Latin textbooks and books explaining how to improve the teaching of Latin spread so widely that they were translated into many European and Asiatic languages. The success of these writings brought him calls from several countries, yet he struggled against poverty a great deal of his life. He was invited to come to Sweden to reform the schools of that country, but refused because he felt that the task was too great for one man. The English Parliament invited him to outline his plans for a research college, but civil war brought an end to that project. He was asked to undertake a general reform of the school system in Hungary, but was prevented from doing more than starting a school there.

Back in Poland in 1654 when Lissa was again sacked and burned, Comenius again lost his library, money, precious unpublished manuscripts, and notes from a lifetime of study. He then went to Amsterdam, where the schoolmasters were jealous of him.

In spite of a lifetime of sorrow and disappointment, Comenius saw in the destruction of the schools of Europe the hand of the Almighty, providing that right foundations could be laid for new ones. Though he had no interest in being radical, he did not want to cling to tradition in spite of the indications of God Himself, reason, and common sense. More than most pioneers of theory, Comenius built his ideas solidly upon actual experience with schools and children, which supplemented his writing through the years.

Comenius was not content to concentrate either on outer or inner factors. He saw a necessary integration of both. His aim was piety, morality, and knowledge. The following is the title page of his major work, *The Great Didactic:*

THE GREAT DIDACTIC

Setting forth
The Whole Art of Teaching all
Things to all Men

or

A certain Inducement to found such Schools in all the Par-
ishes, Towns, and Villages of every Christian Kingdom, that the entire Youth of both Sexes,
None being excepted, shall,

Quickly, Pleasantly, Thoroughly

Become learned in the Sciences, pure in Morals,
Trained in Piety, and in this manner Instructed in all things necessary
for the present and for
the future life.

Let the main object of this, our *Didactic,* be as follows: To seek
and to find a method of instruction, by which teachers may teach
less, but learners may learn more, by which schools may be the
scene of less noise, aversion, and useless labour, but of more
leisure, enjoyment, and solid progress; and through which the
Christian community may have less darkness, perplexity, and
dissension, but on the other hand, more light, orderliness, peace,
and rest.

What far-reaching implications even this one page gives
us! Whereas education had been very narrow, Comenius
would now teach all things to all the youths of both sexes,
a truly liberal education that would broaden their sights
and perspective.

Is it possible to teach pleasantly yet quickly and
thoroughly at the same time? Most schools of that day
could not have conceived of such an idea. This education
was to be "for the present and for the future life." "That
teachers may teach less, but learners may learn more" was
most revolutionary! How could learners learn more if

teachers taught less? Here the emphasis was turned from the teacher to the pupil, who was to become actively involved in his own training. Such education would even have its salutary effect upon the light, orderliness, peace, and rest of the community. These problems are still ours today, and Comenius has pointed the direction in which the answers are to be found.

INNER FACTORS IN COMENIUS

When Comenius sought educational insights from God's written revelation and from the Creator's ways of working in the natural world, he found much that was contrary to the practice of his day. He found that inner factors were being almost entirely neglected. The schools of his day furnished pupils with classical Latin verbiage, but did not train them to observe or to think.

"Development comes from within," he observed from watching the processes of nature. "Nature compels nothing to advance that is not driven forward by its own mature strength." He purposed to work *with* the processes of nature rather than *against* them. Because so little psychology had then been developed, Comenius overdid the use of analogies from nature, but Scripture often compares spiritual growth with natural growth (Psalms 1:3, Psalms 92:12,14, Matthew 15:13, Mark 4:4–8,28, John 15:2), and he saw many valid comparisons. Chief among these is the fact that one grows by his own activity. Teachers and books may help or hinder growth, but the learner must do his own growing. Genuine inward changes are essential for any type of progress for the pupils. "Outward ceremonies without inward truth are an abomination to God," said Comenius.

If a child is to engage in valuable learning activities, he must have a desire to learn, intrinsic interest, and attention rather than artificial incentives. His native curiosity is to be directed into constructive channels rather than repressed. He will be learning as he sees and hears and handles things that are new to him. Why must we use the eyes of others instead of our own? Why aren't we taught to discover for ourselves? The child's room is to be a pleasant place; like a fair, to contain always something new and interesting. How he feels about school has a great deal to do with what he learns in school.

Comenius believed that the wisdom of the Creator Himself was manifest in the way a young child learns before his parents attempt to teach him. The five senses are the gateways to the human soul, the means by which impressions are made on the mind. Therefore the foundations of knowledge should be the child's own firsthand experience with real objects rather than words that are merely symbols of these real objects. The things to be placed before the child are real things, useful things that he may investigate, so that the various senses may combine to reenforce each other for genuine understanding. The teacher should make constant appeal through sense perception to the understanding of the child. The classroom should breathe an inductive spirit. Then things and examples would precede words and rules, and learning would proceed pleasantly from the concrete to the abstract, from the easy to the difficult, from the near to the remote.

On the foundation of the pupils' firsthand experience teaching would be imparting and guiding rather than storing the memory, as had been the custom. Of course memorization is highly important in education, but only the most important things are to be memorized, and then after clear, true impressions have been made on the senses so that the ideas are understood. Learning is by practice as well as by precept. We learn to write by writing, to talk by talking, to sing by singing, to reason by reasoning. In other words, we learn to do by doing. From their earliest years children are to practice the cardinal virtues, to learn self-control rather than simply a superficial veneer of morality.

Therefore the whole person is to be educated. In an

uplifting emotional atmosphere a healthy balance is to be sought between:

> the senses and the intellect
> knowing and doing
> the inner and outer
> deduction and induction.

There is to be plenty of physical activity and play since those are nature's ways of developing a sharp mind and a sturdy body. Because we learn more than one thing at a time, the various senses and faculties should continually be exercised together.

Comenius sensed also the great significance of individual differences. If a pupil does not learn readily, it is not all his fault, but to a large extent the fault of the teacher, who hasn't bothered to find out what he is receptive to or hasn't known how to make him receptive to what he really needs. It is especially essential to introduce spiritual matters in such a way that each one begins to love God rather than to develop a distaste for sacred things.

When Comenius had gone to school, individual recitation had been the order of the day. Each pupil had had to wait his turn to recite to the teacher. "This is a waste of time," thought Comenius as he developed a truly democratic spirit that was not usually appreciated in his day of power politics. Because he felt the need of being able to work with others and to communicate one's thoughts, he formed classes in the pattern of a Latin republic and trained his pupils in self-government and social life.

OUTER FACTORS IN COMENIUS

At the same time that Comenius tried to give individual needs and pupil activity their rightful place in education, he did not minimize the place of the teacher and content. His goals of piety, morality, and knowledge could not be attained by unguided self-expression.

But to Comenius not all knowledge was useful knowledge. Whatever was taught was to have practical application in everyday living. Content was to be selected from the areas of the children's interest. Schools were to be places where children learned to live and work together for common ends. If living and language were taught together rather than separately, pupils would have something worthwhile to communicate, would see the need for sharing, and would use their language for practical purposes.

Since Latin was still considered to be the most important subject and almost the only subject, Comenius tried to teach it effectively by grading texts and methods, and by employing visual aids. When he had gone to school, the boys had taken to class whatever texts they had had at home and had used these to learn their Latin, or had laboriously copied from dictation. Now he insisted that each boy or girl have his own copy of a common text. He himself graded the school into four levels according to the development of the child and wrote Latin texts for these levels. He was a master at organization.

It was Comenius who popularized the picture book for educational purposes, who wrote the first textbook to employ pictures as a teaching device. Whenever he could not bring into the classroom the actual object that was to be the subject of discussion, he used pictures, charts, diagrams, maps, and models.

No wonder he is often called the first modern educator, though he lived so long ago!

Like Comenius, the educators of our own day are striving to achieve a balance between inner and outer factors. They realize the inadequacies both of so-called poor traditional education that seemed satisfied if pupils could parrot back content just as it had been presented to them, and of progressive education that seemed content to provide experience without sufficient guidance by teachers or norms of value. How should inner and outer factors be related in the teaching-learning process? Which should have priority and how should the other be geared in with it?

III

THE TEACHER COME FROM GOD

At a convention of the Evangelical Press Association, A. W. Tozer turned introspective of evangelicalism and recommended four lines of action:

1. Evangelicals need to produce a twentieth-century brand of Christianity that is manifestly superior to any other way of life. Only the old faith will do it. Only a realistic application of that faith to present-day life can make it effective.

2. Evangelicals should call a halt to "spiritual inbreeding" and reach out beyond traditional theological and denominational lines for new life-giving streams of thought and action. Such veins of power are available through fellowship with *all* those who hold to the deity of Christ and the infallibility and authority of the Holy Scriptures.

3. Evangelicals should stop imitating and begin initiating. The world will look to us for leadership when we strike off across the fields of Christian action with a fresh and vital program challenging men of intellectual discrimination and thereby the masses to new heights of vision and accomplishment.

4. Evangelicals need a new emphasis on the "interiority" of the Christian faith, giving less attention to the externals and superficialities of modern Christianity and more to the deeper life hid with Christ in God.[6]

To what source can evangelicals go as we seek to "reach out beyond traditional theological and denominational lines for new life-giving streams of thought and action"? To what source but the Holy Scriptures? When we stop imitating the worldlings about us, on what bases can we start initiating? On what bases but the Holy Scriptures? What will raise us to new heights of vision and accomplishment? What but the Holy Scriptures?

Although the Lord God gave His written revelation primarily to unfold before us His great drama of Redemption, inherent in this library are insights that relate to every aspect of life. Since the Creator-Redeemer is Lord of life, implicit throughout Scripture are His ways of working as well as His thoughts. Action is always carried out by means of some method. If we aren't doing His work in the Spirit by His methods, we're doing it in the flesh by our own methods. The Lord's work done in the Lord's way will have the Lord's supply.

Although the Bible was not written as a textbook of educational philosophy or method, the believer who seeks "buried educational treasure" will be richly rewarded. These treasures are not grouped by categories and openly displayed for the casual observer, but are "hidden" for the earnest seeker who is willing to dig for them.

All of the valid educational concepts that have been discovered through the centuries should first have been discovered by Christians who, like Comenius, looked to the Creator of truth and life rather than to erring mankind. It is He who has made the learner, his teacher, his content, and his environment. Throughout history unbelievers have continually found intriguing new insights into man's behavior because they have taken pains to study God's creature. Long years after these insights have been commonly accepted, Christians have seen the same principles in the Word of God and have belatedly adopted them. Why shouldn't Christians initiate educational progress instead of lagging far behind secularists? We have often been afraid to accept what is solid common sense merely because it has come from godless sources. We have often been afraid to enter into our educational heritage because worldlings have "beat us to it."

Christ Jesus was the Master Teacher par excellence because He Himself perfectly embodied the truth, He perfectly understood His pupils, and He used perfect methods in order to change people. He Himself was "the way, the truth, and the life" (John 14:6). He knew all men individually and He knew human nature, what was in man generically (John 2:24,25). He taught men the truth "as they were able to hear it" (Mark 4:33). Toward the close of His ministry, He said to His disciples, "I have yet many things to say unto you, but ye cannot bear them now" (John 16:12). They were not yet ready to understand and receive them. Not until after His resurrection is it written that ". . . beginning at Moses and all the prophets, he expounded unto them in all the scriptures the things concerning himself" (Luke 24:27).

Does the absolute perfection of Christ tend to discourage any of us who really long to be good teachers? It shouldn't. Of course we could never hope to imitate Him, but that isn't what He is asking of us. He is only asking that we allow Him to live and teach in us. He is asking that His strength be made perfect in our weakness. He wants to have such perfect control of us that He is free to work in His own way through us. After we have diligently studied His Word, He brings to mind the exact parts that we should use. As we study our pupils, He gives extraordinary discernment to understand them. And His own Holy Spirit working through the Word, through the teacher, and in the pupil makes the outer Word an inner experience! Who should not offer himself gladly for such a supernatural ministry!

Students of Scripture sometimes wonder how our teaching today can be compared with Christ's teaching when He never taught in a classroom and we seldom teach outside one. What difference do four walls make? Often they make the teaching atmosphere formal and mechanical, but not necessarily so. A teacher who realizes that only individuals can change and grow will act as informal and make as much use of personal conversation as Christ did. The spirit of the teacher can be exactly that of Christ. He had His own class, the twelve disciples, whom He was training even when He was speaking to others. Even when He was addressing the multitudes, He felt the pulse of the group and spoke personally to them. Many of us who regularly teach in classrooms feel that much of our real work is done outside in casual personal contacts.

A fascinating study is to compare and contrast the way Christ dealt with the Samaritan woman in John 4 with the way He dealt with Nicodemus in John 3. Did He use the same or different methods? Did He use the same or different principles?

METHOD WITH THE SAMARITAN WOMAN
(John 4:1–42)

MAKING CONTACT WITH THE PUPIL

As the Lord Jesus Christ was journeying from Judea to Galilee, He sat down to rest beside Jacob's well in Samaria. His disciples went into the city to buy food. People did not usually come to the well in the heat of the noonday, yet a woman of Samaria came to draw water, perhaps because she wanted to avoid the other women, who scorned her bad reputation.

If you "happened" to have an opportunity to talk to an immoral woman, would you begin by asking her to do you a favor? What was the result of Jesus' request? Put yourself in the place of the woman. How would you have felt if a member of a hostile race asked you to do him a favor? What would you have thought? What did Jesus accomplish by starting His lesson with this personal request?

> He aroused curiosity and questions.
> He aroused interest in Himself as a Person.
> He put Himself under obligation to His pupil.
> He gave her opportunity to respond actively.

What a start for a lesson! In so few words to do so much! The woman had a long way to go spiritually, but at least she now looked at her Teacher with interest and attention. "What goes here?" she thought. "Who is this man and what is He thinking?" The wrong approach would have sent her away indifferent or indignant.

Why were these particular words so potent an approach to the lesson? How is it that the words, "Give me to drink," were full of the wisdom that is from above? The pupil was a stranger, a new pupil, with little spiritual background. Jesus started right where she was, with her own purpose for coming to the well. Since her mind was on water, He spoke to her about water. Since her mind was on her relationship to other people, He showed in these few words that He did not wish to withdraw from her, as did others. On the contrary, He even desired a favor from her. Before Jesus addressed the woman as a Samaritan and a sinner, He accepted her as a person. She no doubt turned from her own musings to look at Him with astonishment and curiosity. This Man was different from others.

Do we Christian teachers start our lessons like this? Do we immediately gain interest and attention? Do we start right where our pupils are, and speak to them of their

immediate activities? Or do we say, "What did we have last
Sunday?" Maybe we think of teaching only as presenting
Bible facts in a formal situation. We don't think of teaching
individuals in the real situations of life. Maybe that's one
major reason why we don't get the results that Christ got.
He didn't need to have a classroom with four walls in order
to teach. He taught His own special class consistently wherever He was, and He taught others wherever He was.

How important is our approach to a lesson? Does the
attitude of the pupils at the beginning make much difference? It is usually the deciding factor. If pupils feel their
need and start with strong interest and attention, that momentum will carry them along and they will become actively
involved. If they are indifferent at the beginning, the
teacher may present a very fine lesson, but he has probably
lost his pupils.

Getting the Pupil Actively Involved

After we have contacted the pupil right where he is at the
moment, how do we lead him to the place where we want
him to go? John 4 gives us the clearest and most skillful
example of this process. With consummate art Christ led
the Samaritan woman in a few minutes from her daily routine to eternal life. Not much of His lesson was a lecture.
Surely the One who was Himself THE TRUTH would have
most right to lecture, but He didn't, not even after He had
gained her attention. He got her to ask the leading question
of the lesson, the question that He wanted to answer! That
is indeed a miracle of teaching method! How did He do it?

Jesus' initial words so incited her curiosity that she questioned, "How is it that you, a Jew, ask a drink of me, a
woman of Samaria?" The Master Teacher had so made His
lesson plan that her curiosity should be directed straight to
the aim of the lesson, that her curiosity should not be
aroused aimlessly. Her question was directed to His Person, so that He would answer it by declaring what He had

come to earth to do. "If you knew," He said, tapping the woman's normal curiosity, and contrasting physical water with living water, "I asked you for a gift of well water, but you could change places with me and ask me for living water."

Of course that response elicited further questions. She wondered how He could get flowing waters of a stream from the deep well when He had nothing to draw with. His answer told her something more about His Person. She recognized that He was making an extraordinary claim. "Who is he? Is he greater than our father Jacob who gave us this well?" This question showed greater seriousness than before.

Though the woman asked the question "how?" the Son of God answered the questioner rather than the question. She must truly desire the living water before she could get it. So He further described it: "Whosoever drinketh of this water shall thirst again: But whosoever drinketh of the water that I shall give him shall never thirst; but the water that I shall give him shall be in him a well of water springing up into everlasting life" (John 4:13,14).

What forceful contrasts between physical water and living water, between thirsting again and never thirsting! The new knowledge that Jesus gave was very closely related not only to what the woman already knew but also to what she was at the moment doing. He did not go on and on explaining eternal life, but waited for her to respond. Her response revealed where she was in the process, and how fast she was ready to go.

When the woman saw the value of the gift that her Teacher offered in terms of her own life, she did not hesitate to express her desire for that gift. That sounds like magic; that will make life easy, she thought. "Sir, give me this water, that I may not thirst, nor come here to draw." She didn't know what she was asking, but His Person commanded her respect as He spoke of a gift that eternally quenches thirst, and could be obtained without effort.

Once the woman herself had asked for what her Teacher wanted to impart, we may be sure that she would listen to find out how to get it. She herself had asked the question that He wanted to answer. From asking *about* living water, she had been led to ask *for* it. Because the Teacher followed her lead and got her actively involved in the process, He had led her from the physical to the spiritual, from her felt need to her real need.

To start with a pupil's felt need does not imply leaving him there, but rather leading him to feel his real spiritual need and then to find the answer to that need in the Word of God.

MEETING THE REAL SPIRITUAL NEED

After the woman of Samaria had expressed her desire for living water, the Lord helped her to see that she desperately needed it, that it was not enough to want it for the sake of ease and convenience. Even in this part of the lesson there was interaction between Himself and the woman.

It may sound as if Jesus is going off on a tangent when He asks her to call her husband, but not so. She had expressed a desire for living water that she knew nothing about. To cause her to feel a need for it, He probed her personal life, which needed cleansing as well as refreshing, by saying "Go, call your husband." When she replied that she had no husband, Jesus exposed her moral guilt. It gave Him an opportunity to use a positive approach while not condoning her actions: "You have had five husbands, and he whom you now have is not your husband. . . ." Earlier in the conversation this bald statement would probably have caused the woman to withdraw, but she was now so much involved and so interested that instead she realized that she stood in the presence of a prophet of God! Who else could describe her life so tersely!

But the conversation was growing too hot to be comfortable. She must divert it from personal implications. She was not yet ready to confess her guilt. So she defended her tradition, by bringing in her own experience as our pupils often do if they feel free to take part in the conversation. She introduced a controversial question that the Jews and Samaritans often argued, whether Jerusalem or Mt. Gerizim there in Samaria was the place to worship God. How often we are ready to discuss religion or theology instead of our personal sin!

In answer to this question Jesus gave the bulk of the subject matter of His lesson. The woman introduced the subject of worship. In His choice of content He followed her lead, telling her that the place of worship isn't nearly so important as the heart attitude, though salvation is of the Jews, for it is based upon God's Word. ". . . the hour is coming, and now is, when the true worshipers will worship the Father in spirit and truth, for such the Father seeks to worship him." Christ gave to this one degraded woman some of the most sublime words, some of the most quoted words ever spoken: "God is spirit, and those who worship him must worship in spirit and truth." He was telling her that genuine worship is personal. And there she was, right back to personal implications.

His amazing answers to her comments, so pointed, so concise, so simple yet profound, were indeed impressive, even to a woman of dull sensitivities. He made her think of the Promised One who would come from God to make known all things. The conversation was raised to a new level of communication, and she expressed a degree of faith when she said, "I know that Messiah is coming, and he will show us the answers to all our questions." Plainly and directly Christ answered, "I who speak to you am he." He had not spoken this plainly to His own people, not even to His disciples.

How far, how very far, the Lord had led this woman in a few minutes! He wasted no time because He started right where she was, stimulated her comments that revealed her thoughts, and went as far and as fast as she was ready to go. He began by referring to her felt need, that of physical water, but went on to talk of living water, her real need. He did not overdo the use of the symbol with which He started. He did not strain it to cover the whole lesson, but kept His content practical and down-to-earth where the woman was.

How often we human teachers speak the precious truths of God's Word into the air because we teach a lesson that is wholly unrelated to what the pupils are doing and thinking! Generalities, even generalities from the Word of God, mean little to most people. If we do not select the part of the Word that meets the personal need, our pupils develop the habit of not listening, or devise their own activities.

PUTTING THE TRUTH TO WORK

When the truth of God meets personal needs, something happens. What do we expect to happen as the result of our teaching of the Word of God? Is it enough to ask our pupils to give back to us the words that we have spoken? Did Christ ask people in the gospels to repeat back to Him His words? What did He want people to do?

So convinced was the Samaritan woman that she had actually been talking to the Messiah, according to His Word, that she forgot her errand to the well, and left her waterpot. Returning to the city, she said to the people, "Come, see a man who told me all that I ever did. Can this be the Christ?" So effective was her witness that people kept coming out of the city to Him. Many of them believed in Him because of her testimony, and many more believed because of His own Word.

What a lesson! And this is the way the Supreme Teacher wants to teach through us today! Even through us!

The result of the lesson was immediate action. Christ taught the woman not in order that she might know something for future use or do something in the future, but in order that she might be changed that day, in order that she might make a definite response in the present. Trying to teach for an unknown tomorrow is usually vague and general and ineffective. If a person finds his deepest needs met today by the Living and written Word, he will be ready to go to the same source tomorrow.

METHOD WITH NICODEMUS

Nicodemus and the Samaritan woman are vivid contrasts. He was a distinguished intellectual ruler of the Jews with strict traditional, ritualistic religious background; she an ignorant social outcast of a mixed race that was looked down upon.

While the Lord Himself approached the woman, Nicodemus showed his readiness for learning by coming to Jesus for an explanation. In his initial comment Nicodemus went straight to the heart of the problem of "this new teacher" by acknowledging who Christ was. He had correctly perceived the nature and purpose of His divine signs, that they had been used to bear witness that the Father had sent Him (John 5:36). Then with a clear, radical statement Jesus set this intellectual to thinking and questioning, just as He had done with the Samaritan woman, only of course on his own plane, on a much higher level, a discerning level. He said in effect, "You have seen signs that no one could do unless He came from above. What you want and what you need to see is the kingdom of God. You can't see the kingdom unless you are born from above. You must have a new life principle. You must have a personal experience with God."

Thus the Lord acknowledged the discernment of the Pharisee, and paid him the compliment of talking on the same high level where he had begun. Not to many people in His total ministry did He commit Himself to speak of the inner transformation of life that He had come to make possible. He followed the lead of Nicodemus in keeping the locus "from above," but probably shocked him with the terse analysis of his personal need for a new experience.

The Pharisee admitted the wonder of this new idea just as he had admitted the wonder of Jesus' signs, but he couldn't visualize how new birth could take place. Here his formal, traditional background held him captive, for he was used to a materialistic outlook in religion rather than a spiritual. What could a birth from above mean? He didn't reject what the Lord said, he was trying to understand, but he couldn't make connections between his conception of God and this revolutionary idea.

So Jesus explained in terms of his background. He first repeated the new idea in different words, using water and the Spirit as the means of the creative purification. No doubt Nicodemus had heard John the Baptist urge people to be baptized with water unto repentance and had heard him say that the Messiah would baptize with the Holy Spirit and fire. Jesus continued, saying in effect, "I'm not speaking of the realm of the flesh, but of the Spirit. This kingdom is from above. It is more than an intellectual idea, requiring more than an intellectual response. But let's illustrate from the realm of the physical. We don't question the reality of the wind though we know its operation only from its effects."

But Nicodemus didn't understand. All his background of intellectual training and religious formalism and educational prestige hindered him from discerning the crucial need that Christ was presenting. Yet in the privacy of the nocturnal interview he implied a desire for it by his further question, "How can I experience this new birth?"

Probably with more sadness than satire Jesus answered, "Are you the outstanding spiritual leader of God's people, and yet you don't understand this focal spiritual experience? If you don't understand from an earthly standpoint the need for a new life principle, how can you understand if I explain the mystery of how it works from a heavenly standpoint? Would an illustration from Moses help, since you rely so much on that Hebrew lawgiver? Just as Moses lifted up the serpent in the wilderness as a symbol of God's judgment on sin, so the Son of man will be lifted up, that whoever believes on him should not perish in his sin but be born of God into eternal life."

The inspired record gives no more of the comments of Nicodemus, perhaps because he made no more.

As the Master Teacher talked to this leader who was responsible not only for his own soul but also for the life of the chosen people and through them for the world, He broadened His scope to make general statements that a leader ought to act upon. The issues were momentous, no less than the condemnation and judgment of the world. But God had provided salvation through the love and light that His Son had brought into it!

Nicodemus strained to fathom the import of these words of authority. How overwhelming and overpowering they must have sounded to him, accustomed as he was to formal ritualism. Yet they came from One who displayed truly divine credentials. For once his intellect failed him. But even if he didn't understand, how could he ever be satisfied now unless he experienced this new life? We don't know how much inward response he made to these matchless words, but we know from John 7:50–52 and 19:39 that he later questioned the denunciation of the Sanhedrin and aided in preparing the body of Jesus for burial.

Thus we see from the interview of Christ with Nicodemus that when an intellectual came to Him seeking an explanation, He did not hesitate to explain logically from the known to the unknown, as did Herbart. He presented the new idea in terms of the old and generalized and applied. Yet His approach was not the recall of a past idea. Rather, He began with the personal need of Nicodemus, and related every part of the explanation to that personal need.

On the surface it may look as if Christ dealt very differently with the Samaritan woman and with Nicodemus. But the basic principles are the same. As with the woman, He started right where the Pharisee was: He took his question right out of his mind before he had a chance to express it. He aroused his curiosity and questions, He stimulated him to ask leading questions, He met his personal spiritual need, He related the new material to old. Since Nicodemus was an intellectual religionist with so much background, less overt interaction was necessary. But who doubts that there was plenty of inner reaction as the interview proceeded?

METHOD WITH THE BLIND MEN

Another rewarding way to study the methods of Christ is to watch Him work with the various blind men who are included in the gospel record. There are four stories of blind men, three of them being described in a paragraph, one constituting a whole chapter. The fourth set of Scripture references may refer to more than one incident that occurred near Jericho, yet the action is so similar that for our purposes we may group them, as do many commentators. Each incident should be studied in its context, or, educationally speaking, in its setting in a curriculum unit.

Matthew 9:27–34	1 paragraph	in a curriculum unit on faith
Mark 8:22–26	1 paragraph	in a curriculum unit on understanding who Jesus was
John 9	1 chapter	in a curriculum unit on insight into His work
Matthew 20:29–34 Mark 10:46–52 Luke 18:35–43	1 paragraph	in a curriculum unit on the first last and the last first

It may seem surprising to speak of curriculum units in relation to the gospels, and of course one cannot be dogmatic about marking off dominant emphases. Yet because Christ showed deep concern both for the people to whom He was ministering and for the content of eternal truth that

He had come to earth to reveal, it is helpful to put these blind men in their educational setting before we begin to analyze their situations.

Did Christ treat all the blind men alike? Because He is Lord of life, did He act in sovereign ways that are past our finding out? Because He could do anything He liked, did He do whatever came to mind at the moment? Or did He show us how to minister to others by providing valid examples and principles? What difference did the readiness of the blind men make? What difference did the curriculum unit make, or in other words, the emphasis that He was currently making? In John 9 when a whole chapter is devoted to a description of what happened to the blind man, why is so much detail included?

Let's look first at the last incident because there the Lord did least. In Mark and Luke He only spoke the word and the blind man was healed. What are we told about the blind man? He was a beggar, in Mark named Bartimaeus, son of Timaeus, which means "highly prized." This is the only blind man whose name is given. What do you suppose is the significance of this fact?

When Bartimaeus heard a multitude going by, he inquired what it meant, and cried out to the Lord, "Jesus, thou son of David, have mercy on me." By this familiar Messianic title he acknowledged who Jesus was. When the multitude rebuked him for bothering the Master, he cried out all the more a great deal. When Jesus called him, he joyfully cast away his outer garment, sprang up, and came to Jesus. In answer to Jesus' question, "What do you want me to do for you?" he said "Lord, that I might receive my sight."

With such a display of readiness and faith, what else was needed? "Thy faith hath made thee whole." Then this poor beggar, for whom the Lord had made the multitude stop, took his place in the crowd that followed Jesus. Do we conceive him bringing up the rear of that group, or would a man with his strong inner drive and his newly found sight be out in front glorifying God? When the people heard his hearty thanksgiving, they too gave praise to God. So the blind beggar who was held in contempt, whom the crowd considered too low for Jesus to notice, now leads His train! The last shall be first.

Note that previous to this incident Christ had taken time to bless children contrary to expectation, had sent away the rich young ruler because he lacked the one thing needful, had foretold the crucifixion of the Lord of life, had rebuked the ambition of James and John to sit on His right and left in the Kingdom. After this incident Jesus went to the house of the hated publican Zacchaeus. In this curriculum unit He seems to be teaching primarily that the first shall be last and the last first.

In Matthew 20:29–34 the blind men also showed great eagerness, but not to the extent that we find in Mark 10 and Luke 18. Here Jesus merely touched their eyes, and they received their sight.

An incident similar to this is that of the two blind men in Matthew 9. Here they followed the Lord, crying out and saying also, "Have mercy on us, Son of David." They actively followed Him into the house. When He asked them, "Do you believe that I am able to do this?" they answered, "Yes, Lord." He often asked people to express their need before He met it. Then He touched their eyes, saying "According to your faith be it unto you."

In a period when the Master Teacher was stressing faith as the requirement for the work of God, the blind men served as an object lesson to demonstrate active faith.

Bible students often question the Lord's actions in Mark 8:22–26. Instead of healing immediately as He usually did, He healed this blind man in two stages. For what reason, when He is able to do anything?

Let's look first at the setting of this incident, which is unusually significant since it precedes Peter's confession of Christ, which serves as the culmination of His whole ministry up to this point. He has explained and demonstrated His signs and their purpose as His credentials, the nature of the Kingdom, the necessity of faith, and finally He leads His disciples to a fuller understanding of who He is. After He has fed the five thousand, the people were about to take Him by force to make Him king when He withdrew into the mountain alone. The disciples could not understand this. Didn't He want to be acclaimed by the people? Soon He repeated the miracle by feeding the four thousand, with no positive response on the part of the disciples. They hadn't learned from the previous experience. When He discoursed to them on the bread of life, some of His disciples walked no more with Him for His words were unintelligible. When He bid them beware of the leaven of the Pharisees, they thought He was talking about physical food.

Therefore in Mark 8:17–21 we have some of the most lamentable words ever spoken by the Lord:

> Don't you yet perceive, neither understand?
> Is your heart hardened?
> Having eyes, don't you see?
> Having ears, don't you hear?
> Don't you remember?

When the disciples came to Bethsaida, they brought to Jesus a blind man and besought Him to touch him, as He had often done to others. What does this passage tell us about the man himself, his faith, his readiness? Nothing at all. He did not come of his own accord, and no comments indicating his inner life are recorded.

At this moment the Lord was just as concerned about the spiritual progress of His disciples as He was about the blind man. He knew that it was time for them to begin to hear of

His coming suffering. But before that shock they had to be assured that He was God's Promised One. It had been a struggle for them to understand His high divine ways, but gradually they had been developing spiritual perception.

So He used the blind man whom they brought to show them how their own blind eyes were being healed, by stages rather than by spontaneous illumination. At first they had seen spiritual things vaguely, but as they companied with Him they finally saw things clearly. Then He took them to a quiet, remote retreat in Caesarea Philippi where He could be alone with them. There He asked them who they thought He was, received the right answer, and from that time began to show them that He had to be killed and be raised up (Matthew 16:13).

Since the blind man himself showed no signs of faith, the process through which Christ led him served to strengthen his faith because of personal contact with the Lord. He took hold of his hand, led him out of the village, spit on his eyes, laid His hands upon him, and questioned him. After the first stage of the healing, He again laid His hands upon his eyes, and lastly gave him an authoritative command. No doubt the faith of the disciples in bringing the blind man to Christ had done something to create readiness in him.

In the section of the gospels that stresses insight into Jesus' work, the Apostle John takes a whole chapter to tell his story of the beggar who was born blind. This time no one asked the Lord to heal the man, neither the man himself nor his friends nor the disciples. Everyone considered his case hopeless. As the disciples saw the man blind from his birth, their reaction was a theological question, "Who sinned, this man or his parents, to bring this calamity upon him?" "Neither," answered the Lord, "but that the works of God should be manifest in him, I'll use him to show how I'm the light of the world." How remarkably the Master Teacher capitalized on every natural opportunity; whenever He found spontaneous interest and attention, He made of it a vital teaching situation.

Jesus spat upon the ground, made clay and anointed the blind eyes with the clay. This activity in the blind man's behalf in addition to His personal contact must have stirred the man's mind and emotions. Jesus then said, "Go, wash in the pool of Siloam." This required the blind man to obey the command of One whom he had never seen. There was something in the manner and the voice and the touch of God's Son that caused the man to go immediately. When he washed, he saw the world of nature and its inhabitants for the first time!

This healing was not the reward of faith, or at least of very strong faith. The man didn't even know who had healed him. But Jesus didn't let him go until his inner spiritual light paralleled his physical sight, until his faith had been developed to the point of true commitment. The man needed the experience of countering unbelief to clarify his own thinking. He needed to be on his own to develop his own convictions after sitting for so many years in a miserable, hopeless condition. So Jesus withdrew from him for a time until he could get that experience.

When the man's neighbors saw him walking about normally, they couldn't believe it was he. When they asked him how his eyes had been opened, he clearly and accurately stated the facts he knew about the man called Jesus, but he didn't know where Jesus was. As he listened to the Pharisees arguing among themselves how a Man whom they considered a sinner could do such signs, he concluded that Jesus must be a prophet, and said as much. His parents were afraid to commit themselves to the Jews, who questioned him a second time. The man told only what he knew, that he had been blind, but that he now saw. Again they asked how Jesus had opened his eyes. This irritated the man, and the Jews reviled him. He then reasoned very logically and boldly with them. "It is a marvel that someone has power to open my eyes and yet you don't know him. Whoever else since the world began has opened the eyes of a man born blind? If this man were not from God, he could do nothing." He had come a long way in spiritual insight into the work of God. But the Jews cast him out.

With perfect timing the Lord then found him and asked if he believed on the Son of God. He replied tenderly, "Who is he, Lord, that I may believe on him?" When Christ revealed Himself, the man confessed his belief and worshiped Him. In helping the disciples gain insight into His work, He gave the blind man physical sight before spiritual sight.

How amazingly the Master Teacher met the personal need of each blind man while at the same time He trained His disciples to carry on His work! How amazingly He used every occasion as it arose to reenforce the particular content that the learners needed!

Why did the "teacher come from God" treat these blind men so differently? Active faith He rewarded without further ado. Incipient faith He developed until it was strong enough to receive the healing that He so willingly offered. Healing always involved the whole person.

As we contrast the methods used with the blind men, it is easy to see why the Lord used means in two cases and not in two others. When the men were not acquainted with Him and His powers, they needed means to develop their faith by personal contact with Him. He made use of physical means not because *He* needed them but because *they* needed them.

Students of Scripture sometimes wonder why the Lord often asked people who needed healing the very evident question, "What do you want me to do for you?" This type of question focuses the personal need, effects a request from the seeker, and reveals the close relationship that is necessary between the Lord and the recipient.

METHOD IN THE PARABLES BY THE SEA
(Matthew 13:1-52, Mark 4:1-34, Luke 8:4-18)

A. T. Pierson has said that "every parable of Jesus was a miracle of wisdom, and every miracle a parable of teaching." In addition to the fact that Jesus' parables fulfilled Old Testament prophecy, we can see many educational reasons for His extensive use of them. Their vivid imagery transported the hearers back into the common activities of their everyday lives and pictured the truths of God in terms of those experiences. So familiar were the problem situations that the audience couldn't help projecting themselves into them, and since they vicariously went through the experiences, they wouldn't soon forget them. People understand best not bare statements, not abstract generalizations, but concrete ideas put into experience and illustration. Today the Lord often uses other people's lives as parables for us.

Because Christ didn't usually spell out the spiritual implications of His stories, He made His audience actively analyze their own problems and learn by their own self-activity. They themselves had to make the application. When they heard such pointed, penetrating illustrations which they sensed had deep meaning, they must have turned them over and over in their minds.

Remarkably adaptable to people of all stages of spiritual development, parables can be comprehended by each according to his spiritual capacity. If a hearer got the one main idea of a parable, he would have a clear impression of that truth. If he were a genuine seeker who didn't get the point, he would no doubt keep it in mind or inquire of the Lord. If he had little or no interest in the Kingdom of God, he would likely walk away without further rejection of the truth at least. As we aid some learners in a group to accept more of God's Word, we don't want to be responsible for aiding others in further hardening their hearts.

In the seven parables that Jesus told by the seaside, we can see some of the salient principles that He used in teaching content. How did He treat this body of content compared with the way we today teach content and compared with the way Herbart taught content? This section of Scripture may be outlined as follows:

JESUS: Gives parable 1
DISCIPLES: Why parables?
          What does this parable mean?
JESUS: The multitudes don't see or hear
       You are beginning to see and hear
       Explains parable 1
       Gives parables 2, 3, 4
DISCIPLES: Explain parable 2
JESUS: Explains parable 2
       Gives parables 5, 6, 7
       Understand all these things?
DISCIPLES: Yes
JESUS: Disciples of the Kingdom produce treasures old and new.

This experience of the disciples may be considered a test on the nature of the Kingdom of God. Up to this time the Master Teacher has been demonstrating and explaining a conception of the Kingdom that was totally different from what they expected. They have watched the King Himself at work. Now He tests the quality of their learning.

What is it that He is looking for as the result of His teaching? Does He want a factual reproduction of the truth, as many of us do? No, He wants nothing repeated back to Him. He says that whoever has some understanding will be given more. "Take heed . . . how ye hear: for whosoever hath, to him shall be given; and whosoever hath not, from him shall be taken even that which he seemeth to have" (Luke 8:18).

But just as Isaiah prophesied, God's people hear without

understanding, see without perceiving, for their hearts have grown dull. They have closed their eyes and ears lest they understand and turn to the Lord so that He can heal them. "Blessed are your eyes," He says to the disciples, "for they are beginning to see, and your ears, for they are beginning to hear." These words indicate that Jesus was seeking spiritual insight, spiritual perception, spiritual understanding.

That's why He was so careful to give His disciples eternal truth "as they were able to hear it" (Mark 4:33). Learning is a process, usually gradual, but marked sometimes by high moments of rapid advance.

In this section of Scripture He first gave the disciples a key parable and explained it when they asked Him to. Then He tried three more. They requested help also on the second. We don't know whether or not they needed further explanation, for Mark 4:34 says, "privately to his own disciples he expounded all things." At the end of the parables at least when the Lord asked them if they had understood all these things, they answered "Yes." Their response and insight told Him how fast they were ready to go.

The insight that Jesus sought was developed by the pupils' own active discernment of the meaning of His stories. One after another He told, challenging their thinking. When they needed help with the first parable, He didn't get discouraged and change to abstract generalization; he used another illustration, and gave them another chance to think for themselves.

This method contrasts sharply with the Herbartian system, for Herbart would have raised the process as soon as possible to the abstract level, and would have given the pupils much less self-activity. Whereas Herbart would have expected the generalization automatically to result in right practice, Christ in His teaching constantly combined parables and generalization and personal experience. In the incident preceding this one He had generalized about His brethren; in the next incident He gave them the emotional experience of a storm on the lake.

METHOD WITH THREE GROUPS SIMULTANEOUSLY
(Luke 15:1—17:11)

How often we have in one class several types of people with very different types of needs! Perhaps there are the unsaved, saved who are babes in Christ, and saved who have gone on some distance with the Lord. We are sometimes dismayed to try to meet all these needs in one short class period. Can it be done? What did the "Teacher come from God" do under such circumstances?

During His Perean ministry publicans and sinners as well as scribes and Pharisees thronged Him and His disciples. Feeling the pulse of the group, He sensed that the hypocritical religious leaders murmured against Him because He received sinners and ate with them. As was His custom He began His teaching right where they were, with their own hostile feelings. He taught both these groups at once by directing *to* the Pharisees three parables *about* the publicans and sinners whom they scorned. These three parables developed sympathy for the lost things, the sinners. What shepherd would not leave ninety-nine sheep in order to find one that was lost? How a woman rejoices who has found one coin that was lost! How the loving father rejoices when his lost son returns!

While the Pharisees and sinners digested those stories that related personally to them, Jesus turned to the disciples and gave them a parable to meet their needs. In the story of the prodigal son they had no doubt identified themselves with the older rather than the younger brother. Jesus now said, "If you have not been faithful in unrighteous mammon, who will commit to your trust the true riches? You cannot serve both God and mammon."

This caught the attention of the Pharisees because they

were lovers of money, and they scoffed at Him. He countered to them, "You justify yourselves in the sight of men. But what is exalted among men is an abomination in the sight of God." At this point we can almost hear the Pharisees arguing, "But we are guardians of the Law."

Jesus answered, "The law and the prophets held sway until John. Since that time the gospel of the kingdom of God has been preached, and all kinds of men are crowding into it. You are hiding behind the law, but you are not heeding Moses." He then told the story of the beggar Lazarus and the rich man in Hades. The Pharisees would identify themselves with the rich man and the sinners themselves with Lazarus. In the story Father Abraham told the tormented rich man that if the Jews would not heed Moses and the prophets, neither would they be persuaded to repent if one rose from the dead.

Again Jesus turned to His disciples and spoke to them about the Pharisees as well as themselves. "Woe unto him who causes others to stumble. It would be better for him to be thrown into the sea than to cause one of these lowly sinners to stumble. Take heed to yourselves. If your brother sins, rebuke him; if he repents, forgive him even seven times."

The disciples then made a spiritual request of the Lord that must have delighted His heart, the only request they ever made for His inner working in their own lives. "Lord, increase our faith," they said. This request went much deeper than their request to teach them to pray. What occasioned this mature response? No doubt the high standard that He had just set for forgiving others. May it not also have been caused by the obtuseness of the Pharisees, who showed no spiritual discernment whatever? Sometimes we human creatures see more clearly our own need when contrasted with the greater need of others. If we must have in one group people with diverse needs, the Lord can use even that situation to further His aims.

It must have been gratifying to the Lord to discuss with His disciples the subject of faith after they had made this direct request. A real teacher likes nothing better than to get a spiritual request from his pupils, for he knows that they are then ready to receive of the Lord. Jesus answered, "If you have genuine faith, though it be as small as a mustard seed, it will grow to be large and conspicuous. You should be able to say to this sycamore tree, 'Be rooted up and be planted in the sea.' But if servants of the kingdom do only their duty, they aren't very profitable. Wondrous things are possible if servants with faith go beyond the call of duty." The disciples then experienced with Him the exciting events of the raising of Lazarus and the cleansing of the ten lepers as examples of what genuine faith can do.

Therefore we see that the Lord taught three types of people simultaneously, meeting the needs of each type. He directly addressed the Pharisees and the disciples about their own needs in relation to the needs of the sinners. He kept all three groups alert and thinking. What a Teacher!

THE HARDEST LESSON THAT JESUS HAD TO TEACH

What was the hardest lesson that Jesus had to teach? God's people through centuries had been led to expect one type of king while He came the first time to be an entirely different type. They wanted a powerful earthly king who would deliver them from all kinds of distress, including the political and economic. He needed to come first as a suffering Savior who would deliver them from personal sin and on the ground of His Redemption enable them to live victorious spiritual lives.

This concept of a spiritual kingdom was much more difficult for the disciples to grasp than for twentieth-century people to grasp today. We live after the historical cross, when the Holy Spirit has been given, when the full New Testament Scriptures are in our hands, when the symbol of the cross is worn as a decorative ornament. Not that we don't have trouble getting people to feel the need and relevance of the cross in their own lives, but at least it has been accepted as part of our culture. When Jesus came to earth, His people were looking for an earthly monarch on a throne.

Therefore the Master Teacher did not immediately introduce this radical new idea, but very carefully led up to it and most skillfully wove it into His curriculum. The way He did this may be studied by following the narrative of the synoptic gospels from Matthew 15:32 to 17:23, Mark 8:1 to 9:32, Luke 9:18 to 9:45.

This section begins with the feeding of the four thousand. Why did the disciples here make no overt response to this great miracle? They merely repeated what they had done at the time of the feeding of the five thousand without any evidence that they had learned from that previous experience. When Jesus remarked that He had compassion on the multitude because they had continued with Him three days with nothing to eat, the disciples said just as they had said before, "How would we be able to fill these men with bread here in this desert place?" They told Him how much food they had, set it before the multitude, and gathered what was left after the meal. That was all. Hadn't the stupendous miracle of the five thousand made any impression on them? How can we explain this lack of response?

After the feeding of the five thousand the people had said in their excitement, "This truly is the Prophet that comes into the world," and were about to take Him by force to make Him king. Instead of accepting this public acclaim, He had withdrawn to the mountain by Himself! The disciples were bewildered. Public acclaim had been exactly what they had been looking forward to. When it came, He refused it. They were flabbergasted! Moreover, when Jesus had discoursed on the bread of life, many of His disciples walked no more with Him, for how they could eat the flesh of the Son of man and drink His blood was unintelligible to them.

After the feeding of the five thousand and the four thousand and all the other miracles, the Pharisees and Sadducees, who should have led God's people in their acceptance of Him, came to tempt Him by seeking a sign from heaven. He sighed deeply and left them. When the disciples reached the other side of the lake, He said to them, "Beware of the leaven of the Pharisees and Sadducees." The disciples reasoned, "He means that we've forgotten to bring bread." But Jesus answered, "O you of little faith! Don't you yet have spiritual discernment? Don't you see? Don't you hear? Don't you remember?" Then they finally "put together" His words and their experience; they finally sensed that He was warning them to beware of the teaching of the religious leaders.

This was the low ebb of their dullness of heart. They surely must have been chagrined by His piercing questions. He was expecting more of them. Yes, His standards were very high. But He had grown emotional because they were not attaining them. Is not their slowness of heart encouraging to us who teach today when our pupils do not readily respond to the truth? Even the Master Teacher in the fulness of the Godhead had to adjust His pace to that of wayward human nature.

The next incident was that of the blind man of Mark 8. As explained earlier in this chapter, the Lord healed this man in stages to show the disciples that inner sight was a process that should be continued until clear vision had been achieved.

Then, knowing that the time had come for Him to begin to mention His death, Jesus took His disciples apart to a quiet retreat. On the way as He was praying alone (He always seemed to be praying alone, for His disciples had little fellowship with Him in this mature occupation), He asked them, "Who do men say that I am?" Then "But who do you say that I am?" Peter as spokesman answered in adoration, "Thou art the Christ, the Son of the living God!"

These words might mean many things to many people. The disciples had already used words to this effect. In John 1, Andrew, Philip, and Nathanael had confessed Him as Messiah. After Jesus and Peter had walked on the water, the disciples in the boat had worshiped Him, saying "Of a truth thou art the Son of God" (Matthew 14:33). In the crisis occasioned by the discourse on the bread of life, Peter had called Him the Holy One of God (John 6:69).

The Lord knew that this confession now meant more than it had formerly, though not as much as it would mean later. He did not hesitate to give Peter hearty approval and to identify the church that He would build with this confession of faith. How must the disciples have felt as He said, "Whatever you bind or loose on earth shall be bound or loosed in heaven"? Just as they were thawing from their previous defeat to the warmth of this new spiritual victory, they heard those familiar words, "Don't tell anybody."

"From that time" (Matthew 16:21) Jesus began to speak plainly (Mark 8:32) to them of His death and resurrection. This first mention of His passion came after a high moment when the disciples themselves had confessed His deity and when He had been able to speak encouraging words to them. Insight into His Person had to precede insight into His atoning work. Human creatures can never understand what He purposes to do until they catch a vision of who He is.

But the disciples were not yet ready to make the connection between His miraculous Person and His ministry of suffering for sin, between the Old Testament as they read it and its fulfillment in a Messiah who had to die before He could return in power. Though the idea of suffering was totally foreign and repulsive to their thinking, they needed to hear the Lord Himself tell them confidently what was going to happen to Him. Otherwise they would later have believed that His life was taken from Him, rather than that He freely laid it down of His own accord. Because *we* live after the cross, we have no teaching situations comparable to this one. At the "outrageous" idea of His being killed, Peter began to rebuke Him. The same man who had just confessed His deity now contradicts Him. Whereas the Lord had just said to Him, "Blessed art thou," he now says, "Get thee behind me, Satan."

Then Jesus went so far as to call the multitude to Him with His disciples and spoke harsh words to them. "If any man will come after me, let him deny himself and take up his cross and keep on following me. For whoever shall save his life shall lose it, and whoever shall lose his life for my sake shall save it. Whoever is ashamed of me in this sinful generation will the Son of man be ashamed of when he comes in the glory of his Father with the holy angels. Some of you shall not taste death till you see the kingdom of God come with power."

Though these words sounded tragic, the disciples were thankful at least for one thing, that He had finally spoken of the glory of His Father and of the coming of the Kingdom of God with power. Those were the things they had been waiting for, and they wondered if He was ever going to get to them. That's what the Old Testament had said, as they read it. Previously it had sounded as if He were abandoning the whole idea of glory and power. But in this context they weren't sure of the force of these words. He was using them in the same breath with being ashamed of Him and losing one's life and taking up a cross! How confusing!

Why did the Master Teacher at this particular time give this advanced spiritual truth about taking up one's cross? Were the disciples, let alone the multitude, ready for it? No overt response is recorded at the end of the discourse. They probably had almost no conception of His words. Any who were interested in Him needed to realize that they would have to be identified with Him in His suffering as well as in His glory. "If you try to save your life from an earthly viewpoint, you'll lose it. But if you are willing to suffer with me, you'll save it from a spiritual viewpoint." This paradox would separate from the company of the seekers those who were merely curious or those who sought worldly power. It was time to prepare for the end those who meant business. His followers would have to be identified with Him in His death.

After a week Jesus took Peter and John and James up into a high mountain apart to pray. These three men probably formed the inner circle of His disciples who were ready for deeper experiences than the others. Here again Messiah's glory and cross were brought together most vividly. As His bodily appearance was transfigured, Moses and Elijah, representing the law and the prophets, appeared with Him in glory and spoke of His decease that He was about to accomplish at Jerusalem. As a cloud overshadowed the disciples, they heard a Voice from the cloud saying, "This is my beloved Son, my chosen; keep on hearing him." From heaven the Father was confirming His anointed One! He was saying "Hear him." They hadn't been willing to hear Him speak words that they didn't want to hear.

As the disciples came down from the mountain, Jesus charged them to tell no one what they had seen until the Son of man had risen from the death. There it was again, those same dreadful words! How could it be that those were the words that the Father wanted them to hear! Even after the vision of glory, He still spoke of death. What could this rising from the dead mean?

The men tried to connect these words with the Old Testament prophecy that Elijah must come before the great and dreadful day of the Lord. "Elijah has come," replied Christ, and they inferred that He meant John the Baptist. "And don't you remember that it is written that the Son of man must suffer many things?"

The next day when they came down from the mountain they found a crowd gathered around their friends. The other disciples had been impotent to do what they had previously done, what the Lord had given them authority to do, to cast out a demon. We wonder if they might have missed the leadership of Peter, James, and John. Again they deserved severe rebuke. The Lord questioned the father of the tormented boy in order to show the urgency of the need and to elicit faith. Then He rebuked the demon. The multitude standing about were all astonished at the majesty of God!

The disciples couldn't understand why they hadn't been able to cast out the unclean spirit. "This kind comes out only by prayer (and fasting)," He said. "To do this you have to be in intimate touch with God." Christ was able of course to heal this extreme case, and yet He kept saying that He was going to die. The disciples were saying that surely He wouldn't die, yet they proved to be impotent. Glorious power and death! He kept putting these two opposing ideas together!

Jesus then took His friends on a secret trip to Galilee where they might again have privacy. Luke 9:43 says that "while all were marveling at all the things that Jesus did," He said again, "Let these words sink into your ears." On the mountain the Voice from the cloud had said, "Hear him." What will He say now? This time it turned out to be worse than ever. "The Son of man will be *delivered* into the hands of men, turned over by God. They shall kill him and after three days he shall rise again." They were exceedingly sorry (Matthew 17:23). Foreboding of trouble was in the air. They didn't yet understand His words, being concealed from them by long prejudice. Usually they felt free to ask Him questions. This time they were afraid to ask. But very soon they were arguing as to who should be greatest (Luke 9:46).

As in the crisis after the discourse on the bread of life, the disciples withstood this crisis also because they had become emotionally attached to His Person and any alternative seemed less feasible. But the Master Teacher Himself had no easy time leading stubborn, prejudiced men to spiritual discernment. The training of the twelve was in many respects His greatest miracle! He had no difficulty healing disease or exercising power over nature. To transform sinful human nature before His resurrection, before the coming of the Holy Spirit and the writing of the New Testament, that indeed was stupendous!

He says to us, "He that believeth on me, the works that I do shall he do also; and greater works than these shall he do; because I go unto my Father" (John 14:12). Are we doing these greater works? Are we expecting the glorified, triumphant Savior to work through us by means of His Word and His Spirit to transform sinful human nature in our day?

Though our local situations differ from those of His day, our basic problems and principles are the same. Are we following Him in our methods as well as teaching His message?

SURVEY OF THE FOUR GOSPELS

When we study intensively all the specific incidents of the gospels, we are able to generalize on the teaching of Christ as a whole. Isn't it amazing that so many details of His work, so many personal conversations have been preserved for us in the sacred record! But of course this is the way we can best learn, by watching the Lord at work and analyzing His methods in concrete situations.

The Approach of Jesus' Teaching

Just about half the teaching incidents in the gospels were initiated by the learners themselves. As people became captivated by His Person, by the authority of His words and the marvel of His works, they came to Him with personal needs of all kinds. How much easier it is to teach when our pupils begin a lesson! When they begin, we may be assured of their interest, attention, and personal involvement. When our personalities reflect the Lord of life and the Word of Christ dwells in us richly in all wisdom and the Spirit of God is working through us, people will come to us also, and we shall find teaching most thrilling and fruitful.

In the half of the gospel incidents that Jesus initiated, He usually started on a personal level. For instance, He found Philip and said, "Follow me" (John 1:43); He made a scourge and drove the money changers out of the temple (John 2:15); He said to the woman of Samaria, "Give me to drink" (John 4:7). He usually started on a personal level because then the pupils connected His eternal truth with their own lives. The few times when He started on a content level, He continually related that content to the lives of His hearers. For example, as He spoke the Beatitudes of Matthew 5:3–11, the disciples would identify themselves with the poor in spirit, the mourning, the meek. Note how many personal references there are in the rest of the Sermon on the Mount (Matthew 5—7). Is there any part of the teaching of Christ that does not have personal reference? To this question many of us would answer no.

The Patterns of Jesus' Teaching

As we look at the patterns of the teaching incidents, we are first of all struck by the fact that there is nothing stereotyped about them. Each is individual because each learner was different, each need different. If Christ had considered content only, His words would comprise His teaching. But overt interaction with the pupils is the rule rather than the exception. Because He started where the pupil was and let the pupil's response and readiness guide the process, the gospel record is full of the sayings and doings of other people as well as His own words and deeds. What He did was determined by what His learners did.

It didn't matter to Him whether He taught the things of God in terms of water or the serpent on the pole, but it mattered a great deal to the woman at the well and to Nicodemus. The truth of God was so much a part of Himself that He could relate it with utmost versatility to any situation in which He found Himself. We know a great deal about the culture of His day because there are so many references in the gospels to the life of that day.

The settings for Jesus' discourses are evident either from the text itself or from the customs of the Jews. The feeding of the five thousand authenticated the teaching on the bread of life. In the treasury of the temple where He spoke the words, "I am the light of the world," stood two colossal golden lampstands, fitted with multitudes of lamps that were lighted after the evening sacrifice. In the midst of this brilliance He spoke the memorable words of John 8:12. On the last great day of the feast, at the solemn moment when the priest brought golden vessels of water from the stream that flowed under the temple and poured it on the altar, Jesus stood probably in some elevated place and cried, "If any man thirst, let him come unto me, and drink" (John 7:37).

Because Christ encouraged questions and often used questions Himself, a problem-solving spirit pervades the gospels. His power and authority stimulated people to come to Him with their problems. Sometimes He Himself took their questions right out of their minds and posed such problems as, "Do you think that the Galileans whose blood Pilate mingled with their sacrifices were sinners above all others? Or those eighteen upon whom the tower in Siloam fell—do you think they were sinners above the others who dwelt in Jerusalem?" (Luke 13:1,2).

His factual questions were for the purpose of crystallizing the need and focusing attention on it in relation to

Himself. He didn't ask people to repeat His answers back to Him. He was looking for spiritual insight and action on the basis of His teaching. He often used questions to get His learners personally involved in the teaching situation and to lead them on into the truth. He also used questions to reprimand, test, and silence His critics. He often answered a question with a question in order to make the learner think for himself. Requests that many teachers would consider interruptions, Christ looked upon as opportunities to counsel and guide.

Christ did not expect that knowing mentally would automatically result in doing. If this had been His philosophy of education the Pharisees would have been His best pupils. There are many instances in the gospels of learning by doing. While the twelve as yet had much to learn, Christ sent them out to heal and to preach in the second period of His Galilean ministry (Matthew 9:36—11:1). At the beginning of the Perean ministry He sent out the seventy (Luke 10:1–24). As the disciples observed His work, He also asked them to participate with Him, such as distributing and collecting the food when the multitudes were fed. The actual extension of the loaves and fishes took place in the hands of the disciples, not in the hands of the Lord who caused the multiplication. Many people brought their friends to Jesus, the water at the wedding feast turned into wine as the servants poured it in obedience to His command (John 2), Peter walked on the water (Matthew 14) and found the tax coin in the mouth of the first fish that he drew out of the sea (Matthew 17), the disciples took the stone away from the door of Lazarus's tomb and loosed him from the graveclothes (John 11). The Lord often required people to obey His word in order to obtain healing, such as the nobleman with the sick son in John 4 and the ten lepers in Luke 17.

In His teaching Christ relied a great deal more upon deeds than we do. Seldom were His deeds unaccompanied by words, and often He taught by word alone. But so often we expect words alone to do the work, though, in the words of Edgar Guest, people "would rather see a sermon than hear one any day." No deed is stronger than the everyday outworking of the Christ-life; genuine Christian character expresses itself in acts of kindness and sacrifice for others. Moreover, if we had more faith, wouldn't we see more of the miracles that Christ performed, even in this age when regeneration and Christlikeness are the greatest miracles?

In many of Christ's teaching situations, outer factors seem to be balanced by inner. Since the Person of the Lord and His words and deeds were such strong outer factors, there are usually considered to be no occasions in which the inner are dominant, but He produced strong inner responses. In quite a few instances the outer outweigh the inner. This fact has implications for the structure of the curriculum of Christian education, as will be seen in Chapter VIII.

One of our most amazing observations from the gospels is the remarkable way in which the Lord achieved both continuity of content and continuity of experience. He met the most diverse kinds of individual needs as they were brought to Him and yet met those needs by means of eternal truth that He was developing step by step. The gospel records present not a haphazard compilation of events, but steady progress of content and experience toward two climaxes: who Jesus was, and what He came to do.

THE RESULTS OF JESUS' TEACHING

What kind of results are we working for in our teaching? What kind of results are we getting? If we ask pupils merely to repeat words back to us, we aren't likely to get more than words. We'll stress memorization of Scripture, surely, but for the purpose of changing life. If we're looking for transformation of life, we'll teach for transformation, we'll pray for transformation, and we'll not cease our efforts until we see transformation.

Christ didn't always see immediate results, and sometimes His enemies gave Him violent opposition, but people weren't indifferent or bored in His presence. The most common results were amazement and belief! How often do we get those? People were also afraid, were silenced; they questioned, they glorified God, worshiped, acknowledged Him as Messiah, understood His teaching. They brought friends to Him, followed Him, spread abroad His fame, and ministered to Him.

Since the Son of God had come to earth in order that men might have life, every contact led His pupils one step or more toward that abundant life. His concern was for the whole person, that each one might be sanctified body, soul, and spirit. Health, wholeness, holiness were closely related. With the coming of the Holy Spirit on the day of Pentecost, the little group of disciples whom He had patiently nurtured during the difficult early stages began to turn the world upside down. "Greater things than these miracles," He said to them, "you will do because I go to my Father" (John 14:12). Are the greater things evident in our lives?

TEACHING AT THE LEVEL OF LIFE

How do these Biblical principles work out in our teaching today? In our planning ahead of time we start with the Lord, to get His perspective on the whole situation. He knows the inner needs of each pupil; He knows our strengths and weaknesses; He knows the forces of evil that oppose us.

But when we begin a class with our pupils, we begin with them, where they are—where they are as whole people, with body, mind, emotions, will, and spirit (which may be dead or alive). Traditional education that aimed to instruct only the mind is derived from the ancient Greeks, not from Scripture. The Greeks thought that man's good soul was incarcerated in an evil body, from which it seeks to escape, that only then can it see truth clearly. This is not a Scriptural concept. The Creator, who made man—body, soul, and spirit—seeks to meet his needs at the level of the LIFE that He created.

Therefore our aims will be in terms of feeling and doing as well as knowing. In Psalms 119 which features the Word of God, many statements exhort us to study, to understand, to meditate upon, to remember God's precepts. But more ask us to love the Word, delight in it, desire it, treasure it. And even more to keep it, obey it, walk in it, live it. We Christians are to be recognized by our fruit, our behavior (Matthew 7:20). Though we say that changes are needed, do we care enough to put forth the effort to make those changes? We must make plans for motivating change as well as practicing change.

Who are the learners who come to us for teaching? How sensitively can we discern the kind of people they are? How do they feel about themselves? We all start life self-centeredly, relating everything to ourselves. Our self-image constitutes our universe, our frame of reference, the grid that screens everything that comes to us. We see things not as they are, but as we are. Does each pupil see himself as made in the image of God, special, one of a kind, just as God wanted him to be, for His particular purpose? If we feel good about ourselves, we'll be secure enough to improve ourselves. It's difficult to think and do right if we don't feel right.

If our pupils come to Bible class with a question that has spiritual implications, they are immediately ready for God's answer. But if they don't feel a need, we are not wasting time if we first motivate a need. We ask ourselves, "What are these people ready for? What matters to them here and now; how does God want to touch them; how can He communicate with them on the deep level of LIFE?"

In order to work with the Master Teacher at the level of life, we teachers need to become skilled in making connections between pupils' needs and the Scripture that meets those needs. We begin a lesson with our pupils' needs, where change is needed. We focus a personal need until it is in the forefront of attention and the pupils are genuinely concerned about it. This involves the emotions as well as the mind. We see that they feel the need sufficiently to do something about it. Then we direct them to the appropriate Scripture, which now speaks to them in terms of daily living.

A good teacher also becomes proficient in wording personal questions so that they are easily understood by the pupils and answered by the lesson content. The answers are not already known to the class, they cannot be answered simply by yes or no. Starting with this kind of personal question, a lesson is off to a good start and will be easy to teach.

Because human nature does not change radically through the centuries and the Bible speaks to the human situation, it deals with basic problems in spite of widely differing cultures. Bible characters must be studied in their contexts, yet their problems are ours too. After examining how David or Abraham solved his problem, we can elicit the principles that were involved. The lesson's memory verse expresses the principle in general terms that we can apply to our lives. The teacher can provide the setting for the pupils and guide them in discovering the essential truths. It is easier and more pleasant for us to carry out ideas that we have discovered for ourselves. If time is limited, the teacher decides what part he should contribute and what part is most important for the pupils to find.

A keen college senior wrote: "I consider myself a committed evangelical, and I understand that to mean that I hold a supernatural faith. I worship a Savior who was once dead, but is now alive, a Savior who said that a proper faith would enable me to move mountains. But what does this signify? I myself cannot testify to one experience in my life and assert that but for the special intervention of God this would not have happened. I have never seen a vision. I have never witnessed a miracle. Controversion of natural law is with me a logical category, not an experiential category. Is it possible to keep declaring and defending a supernatural faith when our experience does not go beyond the natural?"

Too many Christian young people feel like this. They attend church, hear the Word of God, and go out to do nothing about it. The teacher doesn't really expect anything to happen, and the pupils don't expect anything to happen. On the contrary, we should be arranging spiritual experiences for each age group on its own level, and taking advantage of arising needs that are followed by new spiritual decisions and practices.

James 4:17 makes it clear that knowing and doing are two distinct processes. When we teach people new truth without applying it, we are making them worse sinners than they were previously. We should be able to recognize Christians by their distinctive life-style (Matthew 7:20–21). Obedience is even required for further growth in understanding (Psalms 111:10).

A Bible college student was memorizing for an exam far into the night. He was studying the attributes of God with their Scripture references. About ready to give up, it suddenly dawned on his consciousness that this God he had been studying was his own personal Lord who wanted to be his life. Raising his vision to the Almighty, he committed himself anew to his Master, then continued his study refreshed and quickened. Many young people have not formed the habit of bringing their daily needs to their Maker.

If then we want Jesus to teach in His own way through us, what will our general pattern look like? We'll start where our pupils are, with their current needs, help them find God's answer in Scripture, and begin to practice that truth this week. In reference to Jesus John 14:6 uses the words: the _way,_ the _truth,_ and the _life._ People have many questions about the way to gain their goals—the way of salvation, the way to overcome temptation, the way to be filled with the Spirit, the way to witness. God's Book contains all the truth that He has seen fit to reveal from above. The life is the result in terms of daily experience.

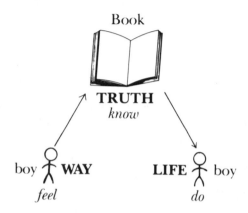

Another way of expressing this general pattern is getting the *boy* into the *Book,* and the *Book* into the *boy.* Initially the boy has no connection with the Book. He needs to get involved in the study of it until it gets into him, until he lives in it and it lives in him.

In terms of our aims for the whole person, we start not with *knowing,* but with *feeling.* Unless our pupils feel a need, unless they want to hear the Word, words may be spoken without communication. But if they want to find the divine solution to a real problem, we'll have no trouble with attitudes. After God's answer, we won't have to preach; we ask: "What should we be *doing;* how shall we respond to God this week? Can you visualize yourself obeying Him? What may be your problems? How can the rest of us help?" And we're ready to pray in earnest.

IV

INSIGHTS FROM OTHER PARTS
OF SCRIPTURE

Are the methods that have been discovered in the gospels peculiar to the "Teacher come from God," or does the rest of Scripture corroborate what is found there? As representative of the rest of Scripture we may select for analysis the Old Testament "wilderness school," Paul's major sermons in Acts, and Paul's epistles. In the Old Testament the Lord God Himself directly taught a whole nation. The Apostle Paul is of particular interest to us because he was a human teacher, called of God and filled with the Holy Spirit, as all Christian teachers ought to be. Though we have his teaching in the form of sermons and letters, pedagogical principles are inherent in them. Though overt interaction is not possible in sermons, and letters do not even require that teacher and pupils be in the same classroom, they have a great deal to teach us in regard to method.

THE WILDERNESS SCHOOL*

Like the rest of the history of the Old Testament, the wilderness school dramatizes with action and color the methods which God consistently used with His chosen people.

Considerably less than the miles from Philadelphia to New York is the distance from Egypt to Palestine. The children of Israel who left their bondage under the mighty delivering hand of God could have reached the new home of milk and honey in a week of comfortable traveling. The time and distance actually consumed in the journey still bear testimony to the ways of God. He whose word could control the forces of nature, take the lives of Egypt's first-born, open the Red Sea and deliver about two and a half million people (Exodus 7—15; Numbers 1), had power to take them directly into the land He intended them to occupy.

But God had long before determined that man's character should be a growth, not a gift. Power would deliver from external forces, salvation would be given, but man must cooperate voluntarily with God to bear His likeness in thought and action (Romans 12; Ephesians 6). From the servitude and degradation and pollution of the heathen, to the pure, lofty ideals which should make the nation a witness to the true God, was not the work of a week. It required wise teaching and much learning. It was therefore no accident that led the people of Israel into the wilderness. It was no accident which kept them there for forty years. There were difficult lessons to be learned before they entered the land of promise to become the cynosure of the world and the pivot of history. They reached Canaan when, and not before, they were fit to settle there.

---

*This section on "The Wilderness School" was written by the author's sister, Mary E. LeBar.

CHOICE OF THE SCHOOLROOM

The location of the school was a part of the planned program. The One who outlined the curriculum was fully aware that learning is integrally bound up with the environment. The learner is profoundly affected by his physical surroundings. Thus the barrenness of the wilderness in contrast with the fertile Nile valley had its part in shutting the people up to concentration upon what God's voice was saying in the schoolroom. He then directed them to the equipping of the schoolroom. Under the towering heights of Sinai, the camp was to be built in an orderly fashion around the tabernacle, over whose Holy of Holies the cloud of His presence ever rested.

But the learner is more profoundly affected by the people around him than by the physical environment. Often it is they who impregnate the atmosphere with emotional qualities which mold the set of heart and will. The same lessons taught in Egypt might have been neutralized by opposing forces appealing to eye and ear and sinful heart, even as the Bible school teacher's lesson may be opposed by the strong influences of a worldly home and school and community. God sought to forestall the negative influences by drawing His people away from the confusion of Egypt into the seclusion where His voice would be dominant. Four hundred years in the midst of heathendom made the wilderness setting essential.

But because that separation was not complete, the mixed multitude among the Israelites still had an appeal that led the people to join them in crying out for the flesh pots of Egypt after nearly a year of training in God's school (Numbers 11:4). For His purpose, separation was more essential than it would be for training in any other phase of life, for the world had its roots within the people, and fallen nature responded readily because of its affinity for evil.

GOD'S TEACHER TRAINING COURSE (EXODUS 2—3)

Eighty years are not too many for the preparation of a teacher for this gigantic task. He must have a thorough grounding in the subject matter he is to teach, and it must be heart knowledge as well as intellectual. There is a vagueness of impression when sacred truths are the curriculum unless there is first a fire burning within the soul of the teacher. More difficult still, the teacher who would influence the spirit must live truth for his words to have weight. If the curriculum is to cover the sphere of the whole man —body, soul, and spirit—in those realms must the teacher's training be given.

Having assured to Moses in infancy the best in secular education, God insured that Moses' most pliable years when permanent habits and attitudes are formed should be spent at his mother's side in a home that, though impoverished, had the riches of spiritual heritage to pass on to its children. The treasures found in the Book of Genesis were doubtless the childhood tales implanted in the mind and heart of the growing boy. The fairylike tale of his own life and the glowing prospect of the future in a palace could not overshadow the promises of God to Abraham which reached the stars and looked forward to the coming of the King of heaven and earth. The sense of values learned in the little hut by the Nile served as a lighthouse when the day of decision came, and meant the choice which was sane only in the light of Moses' early training. The young prince who "chose rather" (Hebrews 11:23–27) did not base his decision upon the sympathy of a movement. The groundwork had been laid in his most formative years.

Moses now felt prepared, in his own mind, for the work of deliverance. His great choice had been made; he would go to the aid of his people. But the most painful lessons lay ahead. The world's school with its knowledge and mental development had failed to teach him the inadequacy of the flesh; in God's school there had to be an unlearning of self-confidence. For the haste of emotion there had to come the deliberate courage of confidence in an ever-present, Almighty One that would keep him true to the trust through abuse, insult, and murmurings without end.

Moses was to be trained in the same schoolroom in which he would teach; he was to precede the class, and for the same length of time. God's course has not yet admitted an accelerated program. Moses had to learn in personal fellowship with God the true nature of the human heart, *his* heart, and the true nature of God, *his* God. These are slow-growing lessons whose fruit is humility toward self and faith toward God. Patience and love for his erring people were not developed overnight.

Even the practical side was evident as Moses learned the geography of the desert and experienced the tent life of the herdsman. When one meditates upon those forty years of personal fellowship with God, in addition to previously earned mental greatness, one understands the simple, quiet manner in which Moses proceeded through a tremendous forty years of service.

Natural Life Situations

In order to raise all of life to a spiritual plane, God's method is ever the spontaneous vitality of actual life. There is no need of artificial stimulation of interest when inner urges are being utilized, when the sources of material are direct and primary. It is true that experience is the best teacher provided it is the right kind of experience, provided it is skillfully guided. The teaching of the children of Israel was closely tied up with matters of the deepest daily concern to them. Hazy abstractions occupied no part of the picture. Learning grew out of their needs and made a difference in their conduct afterward. So natural and informal were the lessons set before these pupils that it is easy to

study them without realizing that they were planned steps
in God's curriculum.

USE OF THE SENSES

Learning was made rich and intense by the full use of the
sense gates. What a constant panorama of color and form
made its deep impressions!

God's people saw manna appear where no food had
been, water gush from a rock and flow over desert sands to
supply the multitude. They saw the mount quake and rock
with fire. They saw the majestic cloud that stopped and
moved, glowed and grew opaque for protection under a
desert sun. They saw the hands of Moses, uplifted in
prayer, bring victory. They saw the order of the camp and
the place of God's abode in the midst. They saw the concrete visualization of evil hearts in the golden calf and its
orgies; the altar with blood poured out for sin.

Their ears heard the trumpet announce the day of travel,
call to battle, the joy of holidays. They heard the thunders
of Sinai and the voice of God which caused them to trem-
ble. From the lips of their long-suffering leader they heard
the rebukes and reproofs that they had to admit were deserved. Their ears detected the quietness of holiness on the
Sabbath rest, and listened in vain to hear the noiseless
manna.

Even the sense of taste was brought into vital relationship with mind and heart in helping to stir proper emotions. There was bitter water and sweet, and manna tasting
like honey and fresh oil. There was also the dust of the
golden calf in their water supply. The feasts and offerings
of the Lord were eaten with gladness.

There was the constant touching of bread from heaven,
of material gifts to express willing hearts, hands placed on
sin offerings in identification, hands busy with careful workmanship on the holy articles of the tabernacle. There was
the forbidding of the touch of the mountain and of the

completed holy arrangement of the tent of God. The continual odor of fragrant incense ascending to God, along with the smoke of the sacrifices, added a perpetual reminder of spiritual facts.

Every gate to the inner man was besieged from without by the lessons to be learned in the wilderness. Every lesson was reenforced, emphasized, strengthened by the senses. No door to the soul was untouched.

REPETITION WITH VARIETY

The farther the redeemed man walks in newness of life, the more he realizes his continuing helplessness, and the less he condemns the Israelites for their ineptness in learning. Over and over the miracles of God's free grace were repeated, not in vain repetition but in accordance with the Scriptural admonition, "precept upon precept; line upon line" (Isaiah 28:10). If secular learning requires repetition, can we wonder that spiritual lessons, opposed by the human heart, come slowly? "God will supply," the manna said. "God will supply," the water at Rephidim said. "God will supply," Elim said. "God will supply," the sacrifices said. Not vain repetition this, for see the march into the Jordan River where neither bridge nor boat was found, in flood season, but without complaint or question. See the march around the walls of Jericho for seven days, without rhyme or reason, but without question or complaint.

Yet repetition was never dull, for the principle of variety was constantly expressed in the learning situation. God's holiness was taught and learned by the bounds set around the mount, by the altar of sacrifice as well as by the laver, by the seclusion of the Holy Place and the Holy of Holies, by the consecration and distinctive dress of the priests, by direct precept and warning, as well as by the death of Nadab and Abihu.

Obedience in casting the tree into the well at Marah brought the desired result. Obedience in picking up enough manna for the day meant sufficiency, while disobedience resulted in stagnation and corruption. The Sabbath exception only furthered obedience. Obedience in giving and building brought joy in the manifest approval of God. Obedience in following the cloud gave the security of guidance; disobedience in entering Canaan in the Lord's time meant forty years of wandering. Obedience to God's way of salvation brought forgiveness of sin; there was life for a look at the brazen serpent.

Every great truth which God set for a lesson to be learned in the wilderness school was presented from so many angles, in such varied ways, that none could miss its import.

INDIVIDUAL DIFFERENCES

Variety was one means of adaptation to individual differences. The spiritually minded might see that the way of life was shown in the smiting of the rock and with the eye of faith might apprehend vicarious atonement. But even the dullest of heart could not miss the meaning of the physical hand placed on the living animal that died with these imputed sins upon him.

There was planning for material as well as spiritual differences. The gifts for the tabernacle varied widely in value. The offerings brought in sacrifice ranged from a bullock for the rich to a turtle dove for the poor; the tithe was based on proportionate income.

Differences in leadership ability were provided for in the men appointed over the tens, over the hundreds, and over whole tribes; differences in wisdom, in the selection of judges to decide disputes. Differences in workmanship were shown in those whom the Lord equipped for building the tabernacle. Even differences in the needs of the heart were taken account of in the range of sacrifices—trespass, sin, peace, burnt, and meal. Differences in age received recognition in special instruction for children. There was to be individualized, personal training for them in each home.

TESTING

"So Moses brought Israel from the Red Sea, and they went out into the wilderness of Shur; and they went three days in the wilderness, and found no water" (Exodus 15: 22). Thus the great wilderness school began with a diagnostic test.

The modern teacher continues to find testing of value. The efficient pedagogue begins to teach by finding out where his pupils are before he undertakes to lead them elsewhere. He needs to measure past achievement to guide him to the proper material and methods. It is fully as important to make the pupil aware of his own needs.

But the diagnostic test is no modern device. God led His people for their first wilderness experience directly to the place where He might prove them (Exodus 15:25). He would determine for their sakes and His own vindication the spiritual location of the pupils. They had in recent days seen His power unveiled against their enemies; they had experienced His grace in deliverance from Egypt. What further proof could be required of His power, His love, His guidance? What would be their response when again, under His guidance, they met a situation beyond human ability to solve? Surely they would turn to Him immediately, they would cling to Him and await His grace and mercy, claiming His promises. But did they?

The answer is full of disappointment. "The people murmured against Moses, saying, What shall we drink?" (Exodus 15:24). Only three days away from the rejoicing by the Red Sea their instability was revealed, their character shown to be woefully incompatible with the grace extended.

Their human teacher, however, had learned that lesson. Moses cried unto the Lord (Exodus 15:25). So began the process of growth by the exercise of faith, a constant exhibition of the patient grace and ample resources of God. His people had begun on the road of that tribulation that works patience, works experience, works hope that makes not ashamed, because the love of God is shed abroad in the heart (Romans 5:3–5).

Then seizing the moment when hearts were assuredly ashamed for their unbelief, the divine Teacher urged them to future right action, adding His promise of health as the incentive most likely to appeal to hearts so manifestly unspiritual. Their thought as yet was wholly centered on escape from suffering. Very well then, they might escape the diseases of Egypt by obedience and right doing (Exodus 15:26). The promise and blessing were followed in close order by the pleasant experience of Elim's palm trees and wells, that pleasure might accrue to the memory of God's supply and His promise. But is the lesson learned?

The second test was one as closely connected with the first as food and water. It hardly seems possible from the vantage point of today that they should not expect that the One who could heal the bitter waters miraculously could supply needed food; that One who undertook to guide felt responsibility for the guided; that love would not forget the loved ones. But unbelief, selfishness and ingratitude are not readily removed from the human heart.

Before long it was lack of water that made the people chide Moses and charge him with bringing them out of Egypt to kill them. God's mercy then opened the fount of water from the rock (Exodus 17:1–7). At Sinai the people revealed that they still did not know themselves when they readily offered to do all the Lord should command (Exodus 19:8).

And so the testing went on, in one form and then another, continually manifesting the true state of progress and the magnitude of the need. The diagnostic process came to a climax in the tables of stone (Exodus 20), which remain as the enduring measuring rod by which all human hearts since have been able to learn their utter inadequacy before God. How few are those who have faced the fact without some bitter trial in a wilderness school!

But testing which denotes failure is not God's final word to any man. Knowledge of self is only the prelude to knowledge of salvation. God's diagnosis always provides a satisfaction for the need revealed (Romans 6:23). Failures in His school are voluntary, not excusable.

The building of the tabernacle was also a test (Exodus 25 —40). What joy followed the successful completion of God's directions! What fellowship, and what appreciation of His presence! Israel had its taste of achievement and approval, as well as of grace. Testing should be a positive technique for both teacher and pupil.

DIRECT INSTRUCTION

Most of the learning experiences of the children of Israel were accompanied by direct instruction or warning, to emphasize the lesson or point up its principle for future guidance. But the giving of the law on Mount Sinai would perhaps most nearly correspond to our stated lectures or book instruction today. That it was a successful method may be understood by a brief analysis of its presentation (Exodus 19—40).

Note first that receptivity was carefully provided for. The people were given the opportunity to accept or reject God's law. Their willing affirmative put them in a yielding, receptive frame of mind. They were prepared to hear His words with the intent of doing them. Their own choice made it a personal matter to hear and do. This was an emotional set favorable to attention.

The physical man was likewise prepared in such a way as to intensify the heart reception. The people were told to wash themselves and their clothing before presenting themselves before the mount. Three days were to be given to this preparation in order that all might not only be clean but also be at ease.

Clean and clothed, anticipative of a revelation from God, the people's calmness was shattered by a tremendous quaking, thunders, fire, and cloud which heralded the presence of God. Those who had seen the terrible plagues in Egypt and the wonders of God now shook before His voice. Awe and fear prepared their minds to receive the words of God not lightly, but as the very words of the Almighty One whose judgments are as real as His mercies.

The holiness of God was twice impressed upon them by the warning to remain at a distance from the mount. Little wonder that the law of God assumed a significance that has survived the years. No less than such a degree of readiness was essential when every aspect of life was to be regulated, lifted to higher planes than any then known, above the strong bonds of habit, above the ordinary mode of life that the eye had impressed upon the soul.

That such renovation was difficult is seen in the rapid lapse when leadership was absent. Then that which had been seen through childhood and youth showed its strength; the golden calf rose in their midst, bringing the habits and practices associated with it.

The success of the law lay also in its character. It was vital. It entered into every phase of life, definitely and directly. Having no other gods meant making no idols. Keeping the Sabbath day meant doing no work. Coveting was defined. Pupils often fail in the application of new principles or in the generalization of a definite experience, but God prevented such errors by definite applications and inclusive generalizations. There was moral law for the regulation of heart and mind and spirit; there was civil law for community and social life; there was ceremonial law for matters of worship.

The law was not a lesson to be memorized and repeated on request; it was a lesson to be memorized for use every moment of every day. The man who picked up sticks on the Sabbath met death because his action showed contempt for the decrees that had just been proclaimed. The effect of this early example was to forbid trifling. God's people were to be holy. Every man could find satisfaction in attaining righteousness through the sacrifices; but he could also expect stringent punishment for voluntary failure.

THE WHOLENESS OF LEARNING

While the fulfillment of promise and illustration today adds limitless depths to the wilderness experiences, the Israelites themselves must have experienced a rich store of associated learnings. Each experience which yields one truth has others attached to it, for truths, like evils, tend to "hook and eye" together.

The manna (Exodus 16) may have had its chief teaching directed toward faith and dependence upon God, but covetousness was curtailed in the gathering of only a day's supply, the folly of hoarding was prevented, pride was leveled, temperance taught, diligence and industry encouraged.

The unprovoked battle with Amalek taught more than the power of prayer as the source of victory, for Israel learned also that hatreds linger long in the human heart; that there would be constant warfare with certain forces; that some evils are better stamped out than tolerated; that separation from the world unto God means alignment with Him against His enemies and persecution because of His favor.

The provisions for the healed leper went beyond hygiene to matters of faith, for who but God could heal the leper? The union of cleanliness of body with holiness of spirit impressed the oneness of body, soul, and spirit, and the influence of the physical upon the spiritual. Learning is change which affects the person's whole complex being; attitudes and habits are being learned at the same time as facts.

PROJECTS

The building of the tabernacle (Exodus 35—40) was a shining example of the project method. Few school projects achieve the reality of this ancient illustration. The building of the tabernacle was accepted willingly and wholeheartedly by the children of Israel as their own activity, as evidenced by their giving and the rapid accomplishment which admitted no need for reproof, but only praise.

The activity was carried out by the pupils under the guidance of their leader with satisfying results. It emphasized right values, compelled thought, sustained interest, and helped to form correct habits of conduct. Had not the people felt a need for a focus in worship, and thereby erred in making the golden calf? Was there not evidence that earlier experiences had really taught increased faith and joy in God, as loving hands piled up gifts for His house? Did not their prompt and accurate obedience indicate that they had begun to learn the importance of obeying? What a joyful experience for both teacher and pupils!

Many were the educational values implicit in the project. A variety of abilities was required, both in men and women, to weave the fine linen and sew it, to dye cloth blue and scarlet and purple, to prepare goats' hair and rams' and badgers' skins, to find shittim wood and cut and carve it, to press oil from olives, to mix sweet incense by a particular formula, to cut precious stones, to mold and cast the metals.

The list of occupations represented gives ample scope for the wide differences in interest and ability. There were quiet work and physical exertion, appeals to the aesthetic nature and the practical, expensive and inexpensive gifts that were time consuming and that were not, gifts requiring skilled and unskilled labor.

By full participation, all the camp became personally involved in the tent-making and more intimately related to the One for whom they built. There must have been an intense personal joy and thrill at the sign of His pleasure when He filled it with the Shekinah glory.

What discussions of purpose and meaning must have filled the thoughts of those who worked on badgers' skins to cover all the glory and beauty of the inner sanctum from the eyes of men! What a pondering over God's way of beginning with the inner room and proceeding outward, while they worked inward from the outside. What questions from children must have resulted in searching for God's meaning in requiring one door, and only one, for the great camp, a door which led first to an altar where blood was to be constantly poured out! An intelligent and questioning people must have sought and found, even though they saw but dimly, as in a mirror, the glory of the Lord, some of the tremendous depths of meaning which the Lord Jesus Christ has revealed as inherent in that building.

What better activity could challenge them to think and search into God's ways and character? Did they not form a broader concept of God as One who loves beauty, who is not above receiving the puny service of man's hands and heart, whose love and interest intrusted them with infinite truth? Did He not thus stretch their minds and hearts and turn them upward in a new realization that they had not yet begun to unravel His mysteries?

The tabernacle was not the only expressional work undertaken by Israel under the guidance of their leader. There was the taking of the census, which called forth the mathematicians and the scientific-minded; there was the ordering of the camp. These too were successfully completed undertakings, with many concomitant learnings. To see the increase from seventy people who went down into Egypt, to this great and growing nation, could only inspire awe for the God who had made them His particular care. Their labors emphasized that He was a God whose character required that all things be done decently and in order. It was also clear that He condescended to take them into partnership with Him in His work.

USE OF QUESTIONS

The exact and willing obedience sought by God does not mean that He is a repressive Teacher. The frequent murmurs of the people indicated the freedom they felt to voice their feelings; punishment fell for the unbelief and sin which lay behind the murmuring. "What shall we drink?" "What shall we eat?" "Is the Lord among us or not?" they cried. Thus Moses knew their true spiritual state so that he could begin where they were to lead them onward. God led in questioning before introducing the law. The frequent conversations between God and Moses set the example for the people's relationship with Him, not to be that of Taskmaster and servants, but of loving Teacher and confiding pupils.

The Jewish child was expected to ask questions as he watched the ceremonies and rites and feasts. He was not taught to be "seen but not heard" in his home. At the Passover, the first of the holidays instituted, the children were sure to ask, "What is the meaning of this service?" (Exodus 12:26); so the parents were provided the answer in advance. When the first-born was redeemed by a lamb, the son was expected to ask, "What is this?" (Exodus 13: 14). In time to come the son was expected to ask, "What mean the testimonies, and the statutes, and the judgments, which the Lord our God hath commanded you?" and the answer was given, clearly and pointedly (Deuteronomy 6: 20).

Moses' farewell song suggests that even adults should ask their elders about the works of the Lord in the past (Deuteronomy 32:7). Parents were to be prepared to answer questions. A heart full of the knowledge and love of God welcomes questions concerning Him. The spirit which

is to discern must have its faculties exercised by use
(1 Corinthians 11:31).

DISCIPLINE

The Israelites quickly learned that freedom from Egyptian bondage did not mean complete lack of restraint. They were allowed freedom of choice even in matters which seemed to involve a risk (Exodus 19:5; 15:26), yet they were not left to make their choices in ignorance of the consequences. *If* they would hear the law and keep it and turn to God, all would be well (Deuteronomy 30:10).

Exhortation and appeal were added to proofs of love and mercy and patience. The very love of both heavenly and earthly leaders led to more severe reproof, rebuke, and punishment. Lack of self-knowledge has ever deceived people into the belief that complete freedom could insure happiness.

One of the notable examples of training in self-discipline came with the giving of the manna. It meant rising early; it meant labor; it meant daily labor, not by spurts when the mood was favorable. Yet even this daily habit was to be under control, so that twice as much was gathered on Friday and none on the Sabbath. There was to be regulation of labor, for no food could be kept overnight, with the one exception. The unbelievers who tested the rule found it true.

There was thus a constant check on self-will. Inner restraints on fallen nature come hard. The first experience after reaching the wilderness, at Marah's bitter waters, ended with the promise of physical health upon obedience, which could come only through self-control.

The tabernacle required willing gifts, which meant heart-discipline. In the bounds set around the mountain at the giving of the law there was restraint upon curiosity, while the completed revelation may be viewed as constant discipline to conform mind and heart to ways above the natural ways of man. The moral and ceremonial and civil laws meant a discipline of the entire life, which in God's plan was to perfect the nation in holiness and make it His witness to the world. No one-sided discipline was this, of outward conformity alone, but the curbing and directing of every phase of life for harmonious development of all the powers.

Discipline in the sense of correction and punishment was necessary too. Fiery serpents seemed just recompense for a people who would speak against God and Moses, complaining and murmuring after years of miracles of love and grace (Numbers 21:5–9). When the punishment fell, there is encouragement in noting that this generation had at least learned to recognize cause and effect, as their fathers who came out of Egypt did not. "We have sinned," they said to Moses, "for we have spoken against the Lord, and against thee; pray unto the Lord, that he take away the serpents from us." They had learned the technique of solving problems, too. Not in vain had been the lessons of the past thirty-nine years.

Here the usual pattern of man's vindictive punishments ends. Man metes out what he considers to be justice, and reconsiders only if this justice is questioned. But God demonstrates the course of divine discipline. The people have sinned, judgment has fallen, but they acknowledge their sin and ask mercy. He extends mercy because the lesson has been learned and continued punishment will not further the cause for which the school exists—the pupils' improvement.

RESULTS

The wilderness school is seen to have offered a choice curriculum for the full and rounded development of every phase of life. Every teaching and learning experience was a part of real life, with purpose and meaning. To take even a cursory glance at the Scriptures assures us that there was provision for the development of the whole man—spiritual, mental, moral, emotional, physical, social.

Because the spiritual man is the principal objective of the entire curriculum, his development underlies most of the preceding discussion. The mental man also had full provision. No mental sluggard could keep pace with the when and how of feasts, the when, how, where, and which of the many laws to be applied in daily life. The moral man found ordinances and statutes that so regulated his life as to leave no loophole for self-indulgence.

The emphasis of modern education upon the emotional man invites attention. Here too God made adequate provision. The difficult lesson of Marah was followed by the peace and quietness of Elim, where rest had time to offset the disturbed morale, to encourage the anxious with its sufficiency, to supply needed fortitude to go on. The Sabbath rest was another outstanding builder of mental and emotional health. The stated feasts gave outlets for joy and praise; even appropriate grief for sin was channeled into a Day of Atonement ending with forgiveness and peace. Outdoor labor brought the benison of physical health as well as the satisfaction of worthwhile accomplishment apart from the strain of competition. The judgments and awe-inspiring spectacles stirred the fear of the Lord which prevents sin, balanced by the constant manifestation of His love and grace. The emotional man found outlet for the normal range of expression.

The physical man, in addition to daily labor caring for flocks and herds and tents, had an active role in worship as he built the tabernacle and took his offering to the altar, an active role in the feasts when the drama of the Passover was enacted or the first fruits were waved before the Lord, an active role in gathering his daily food, an active role in his journeying under the pillar of cloud and fire, an active role in battles.

The social man began to develop in a home life where a large family was the blessing of the Lord. He worshiped in the company of his people, united in common labor for daily bread, celebrated his feasts with others, cooperated in tasks for God. Economic and labor laws taught him new ideals toward his fellow men. Care of the poor, the stranger and servants, as well as tithes, offerings, and service for the Lord developed a deep social sense. The equality of privilege in his nation kept his citizenship a responsible and self-respecting one. Though called a nomad, his was a social life.

In addition to the development of the whole man, the wilderness school sought to establish and emphasize a center around which this developing personality could be integrated. The Lord was the center around which all else revolved. The moral and spiritual must control the mental and physical.

Judged in the light of modern standards of aim and method, the wilderness school was a success. Moses had the advantage of not being confined to ill-built schoolhouses or being restricted by customs and unchanging curriculums. Hence he could do what modern teachers advocate but rarely can practice. He could meet daily needs as they arose. That desired results in some measure were achieved is not therefore a matter for wonder. The wonder is that more immediate, complete, and unqualified success was not attained. What accounts for the recurring failures?

Analysis of each failure puts the finger upon the same sore spot. It lies not in the teaching, but within the pupils themselves. Lessons addressed chiefly to the spirit of man meet the unhappy reception that fallen nature has ever given. Every great testing of the human race in God's school has resulted in failure. There must be a recognition of the limitations of man with his inability to master self fully. Pride and self-sufficiency are the greatest hindrances to educational progress.

Yet the instruction of Sinai did lift and exalt and transform a nation of slaves into a compact, cultured nation living on a moral and spiritual plane higher than that of any other people. When one considers the antagonism of the human heart, the strength of habit and early experiences, this is a large measure of success. An ignorant, untrained multitude left Egypt. They went into Canaan as God's people—keeping His laws, believing His word, welded into an army that obeyed Him—and they gained victory.

More important still, a basis for cooperation with God had been established. God had first place in the nation.

PAUL'S MAJOR SERMONS IN ACTS

The student of Scriptural method is particularly interested in the work of Paul because his situation is comparable to ours today. He was a human teacher who was called and mightily used of God. Though we have Paul's teaching chiefly in the form of sermons and letters, we can elicit from these his principles of method. Though overt interaction between teacher and pupils is impossible in these forms of teaching, we can discover to what extent the hearers and readers made a difference in what he said.

Consciously or unconsciously some Christian workers take the attitude that since all men need the gospel of the grace of God, our human responsibility is to give it out in its pure essence and leave the Holy Spirit to do the individual work in the heart of the hearer. Since the Spirit knows the heart and we do not, we can preach the same sermon and teach the same lesson to all kinds of people in all kinds of circumstances. Our responsibility is to present the Word of God clearly and logically.

Is this what Paul did? The answer to this question is found by comparing and contrasting his major sermons in Acts as outlined on pages 112, 113. Paul's great burden was to witness to the power of the risen Savior to forgive sin, yet notice how different in each case are his tone and approach. His content is also different except in the case of the last two (Acts 22 and 26) when he uses the same facts of his conversion but in quite a different spirit. To what extent did he present the pure essence of the gospel in each sermon? To what extent did his audience determine the selection of his content, his approach, his tone?

The audience that had least background for the good news of Christ was the august council of Greek philosophers at Athens. What folly it would be to think of using this sermon for any of the Jewish groups! In the intellectual and artistic capital of the world Paul was impressed by the religiosity of the intelligentsia and yet by their religious ignorance. Therefore he had to begin back at the very beginning with the one God as Creator, Sovereign, and Father in contrast to their many mythical gods. He went only as fast as they were ready to go and got only as far as the concept of God as Righteous Judge, which was in keeping with the sermon's setting in the court of judgment. He proclaimed that God would judge the world by a Man whom He raised from the dead. The very thought of resurrection was as obnoxious to materialistic Greeks as to ritualistic Jews.

This sermon on Mars' Hill was no doubt a sample of Paul's approach to cultured pagans just as the message at Pisidian Antioch was a sample of his approach to synagogue audiences, and his Ephesian message to Christians. In Athens his quotations were from Greek poets rather than Hebrew prophecies though his argument and language were, as always, securely grounded in divine revelation.

Paul's farewell sermon to the Ephesian elders is distinctive in that it gives his first recorded words to the Christian church. In this discourse he did not spend time laying again the foundation of deliverance from dead works for those who had already received the whole counsel of God, but he urged them to take the next step and warned of dangers to come.

The sermons in Acts 13, 22, and 26 are all addressed to

people with Jewish background who needed the gospel. Those in the synagogue at Antioch were probably typical Jews, with a few Gentile converts whom Paul is careful to include in his presentation. The mob in Jerusalem that was ready to tear the traitor to pieces had experienced the tremendous events that had taken place in relation to the death and resurrection of Christ. Agrippa was a fickle politician who claimed through his early years that he was a Jew. Paul said that Agrippa knew Jewish customs, questions, and prophecies, and that he believed the prophets (Acts 26:2,27).

In the synagogue, after the customary reading of the law and prophets, Paul spoke objectively of the glorious history of his people and the fulfillment of the prophecies. By starting with the story of God's past favors to His chosen nation, he identified himself with his audience and got them to agreeing with him. Because he didn't go too fast nor too far, he could mention God's new favor without arousing anger. God's Holy One, whom He would not allow to see corruption, could justify them from every charge from which the law of Moses could not justify them. Because he let the people's readiness guide him, many of them questioned and sought to hear him further.

Though the Jerusalem mob had the same background as the synagogue congregation, Paul didn't use the same tack with them. They were so bitter that he tried to calm their emotions by showing them how he had felt the very same way and how only God Himself had changed him. His appeal to all that was near and dear to them allowed him at least a brief hearing.

The subject matter of Acts 22 and 26 is practically the same, yet each is adapted in focus and style to its own audience. To the furious Jews on the steps of the barracks, the battered Apostle spoke in the Jews' own vernacular of the law of our fathers, the God of our fathers, and referred to Ananias as a devout man according to the law, well

Acts 13:16–41	Acts 17:22–31
AUDIENCE	
mostly Jews, some Gentile converts ("you who fear God")	Greek philosophers and leading citizens
PLACE	
synagogue at Antioch in Pisidia (Galatia)	Athens, intellectual and artistic capital of the world, on the west of the acropolis before the august council of Areopagus
AIM	
to show how the prophets and psalms have been fulfilled in Jesus, in whom is forgiveness of sin	to present the living God in contrast with Greek polytheism
TONE	
respectful of Jewish background and values, yet firm and forceful	authoritative yet diplomatic
APPROACH	
"We all agree that God has always had special dealings with His own people."	"Since you crave new ideas and are very religious, I proclaim to you the nature of your 'unknown God.' "
CONTENT	
God's past redemptive favors to His people God's new favor prophecy of the Savior from sin appeal and warning against rejection	God as: Creator, distinct from His creation Sovereign of heaven and earth, who dwells in temples not made with hands Father of the first man, from whom all men sprang (not Greeks from the soil of Attica, as they say) Righteous Judge of the world by His Man whom He raised from the dead
DISTINCTIVE FEATURES	
after the customary reading of the prophets, explanation of their fulfillment and also, of the psalms inclusion of the Gentiles in "everyone who believes" use of the phraseology of the Septuagint O.T. with which the audience was most familiar Christianity as the logical outcome of the Jews' own history	Paul's indignation at the Greeks' idols rather than thrill at their art impossibility of representing God by artistic images Paul's authoritative proclamation of the living God rather than philosophical speculation quotations from Greek poets

Acts 20:17–35	Acts 22:1–21	Acts 26:2–23
elders of the church at Ephesus	infuriated Jewish mob	King Agrippa, his sister Bernice, Roman governor Festus, court of Festus
Miletus, on seacoast of Ionia about 36 miles south of Ephesus	Jerusalem, on steps of barracks as Paul was being rescued by the captain of the garrison	Caesarea, at a formal state occasion with great pomp at the court of the Roman governor
to exhort the elders to give themselves wholly to feeding and building up the church	to meet the charge of apostasy from the Jewish faith	to explain the hostility of his people and to witness to the court
tender and practical	sympathetically confidential and apologetic	dramatically magnificent
"I'm not asking you to do anything that I haven't been an example of."	in their own Hebrew language, "I am one of you. I used to feel just as you do."	"I am fortunate to be able to defend myself before a king with such knowledge of Jewish customs and problems."
example of Paul's selflessness and wholeheartedness expectation of afflictions for Paul and difficult times for the church exhortation to feed and build up the church by the word of God's grace warning of future false teachers	Paul's strict Jewish background his wonderful inner experience near Damascus his drastic persecution of The Way the Lord's command to leave Jerusalem and go to the Gentiles	the cause of the furor—Paul's belief that the promises of God to his fathers have been fulfilled his radical opposition to the name of Jesus the majestic heavenly vision his arrest for obedience to this vision
Paul's personal habits of life among them atmosphere of mutual affection and admiration at his farewell disclosure of his inner stresses and premonitions deep concern for their future	silencing of the mob when Paul began to speak in their native tongue appeal to the emotions rather than to the intellect appeal to what was dear to their religious nationalism fresh fury at the mention of going to the Gentiles	loftiness of thought and language content similar to Acts 22 but more rational a broader perspective emphasis on Jewish authority and prophecy more emphasis on the Gentiles emphasis on the need for repentance, light, power

spoken of by the Jews who lived in Damascus. To his rabid countrymen he stressed his education in the strict manner of the law of their fathers in that very city of Jerusalem at the feet of its eminent teacher Gamaliel, and his zeal that had been comparable to theirs in persecuting the followers of the way, as the chief priest and the whole council of elders bore witness.

In the court of the Roman governor, Paul gave this same testimony with a dramatic flourish worthy of its elegant setting. This time he used the Greek language—a polished, literary Greek befitting his audience. To rulers who had arranged a state occasion to hear his defense, he explained the logic and purpose of his actions in clearly reasoned sequence. With rising feeling he built his evidence to a climax. "At midday, O king, I saw on the way a light from heaven, brighter than the sun. The Voice from heaven said, 'I send you to open the eyes of the people and the Gentiles, that they may turn from darkness to light.' Wherefore, O king, I was not disobedient to the heavenly vision. For this the Jews tried to kill me. Yet I've said only what Moses and the prophets said would come to pass, that Christ must suffer and rise from the dead to proclaim light to the people and to the Gentiles." After identifying himself with the strict sect of the Pharisees and the authority of the chief priests, he showed that he was merely being obedient to a higher authority than that of the Jews.

From the results of Paul's sermons we may infer the inward interaction that must have taken place while he was speaking. After he mentioned to the Jerusalem mob his commission to the Gentiles, they wouldn't let him speak further. We don't know whether or not he had finished in Athens when the philosophers mocked at his reference to Christ's resurrection. The Ephesian elders wept and embraced him. So moved were the Jews at Antioch that they talked about his sermon until almost the whole town came to hear him on the next Sabbath. So forceful was the defense in the Roman court that the rulers felt uncomfortable personally.

Paul's sermons kept so close to the personal experience of his hearers that inner response was inevitable.

PAUL'S EPISTLES

(The Book of Hebrews is not included in the list of Paul's epistles; though many scholars attribute it to Paul, its authorship is uncertain.)

Twenty-one of the twenty-seven books of the New Testament canon are letters! They are all letters except the first five and the last book, the gospels of the life of Christ, the Acts of the Holy Spirit in the formation of the new body the church, and the final revelation of the Son of God at the consummation of the ages.

Christ Himself merely mentioned the fact that He would build His church, but left church truth to be communicated to the world by His faithful servant who showed by his life as well as by his words that "to me to live is Christ" (Philippians 1:21). Most of the New Testament epistles were written by Paul, whom the Lord prepared in a signal way to fill full His written revelation (Colossians 1:25). He was trained both in Hebrew and in Greek learning, he was called by the Lord's own voice from heaven (Acts 22:6–11), was personally instructed by the Lord Himself in Arabia where Moses was also taught (Galatians 1:15—2:6; Ephesians 3:2–4; 2 Corinthians 12:1–4).

Isn't it interesting that the Lord has chosen to give His people the whole body of church truth in the form of letters! Most of Paul's letters are not carefully structured essays but informal messages with very personal elements. They are usually addressed to particular churches or individuals, often in answer to letters received. Each one, except perhaps Ephesians, was written first of all to meet very real local needs as well as eventually to meet the needs of the whole church age. Statements of doctrine arise from the nature of the local circumstances.

In the case of some of the letters it is difficult to outline the order of subjects, for Paul sets down his ideas as they come to him. He goes from one to another as we do in conversation, no doubt visualizing his reader and responding to the questions or comments that he would naturally make. His heart is so full that his thoughts jostle each other and often come tumbling out in emotional exclamations rather than intellectual dogmatics. His eloquence stems from spiritual vigor and elevation of soul rather than from artistic polish.

Note the specific reasons why Paul's epistles were written:

Romans—Since Phebe is journeying to Rome, I'm sending with her this announcement that I, the apostle to the Gentiles, hope soon to visit the center of the Gentile world. I'll prepare you for this visit by sending you my logical statement of the heart of the gospel, personal salvation by grace through faith.

1 Corinthians—I'm glad to answer the questions that you asked me in your letter, but "the house of Chloe" reports more serious matters of church conduct than those.

2 Corinthians—As the result of reports of your condition by Titus, let me encourage those of you who were pained by my first letter, and vindicate my character and apostleship for those who do not yet accept me.

Galatians—I marvel that I so soon have to defend my apostolic authority and the true gospel of justification by faith as opposed to the works of the law.

Ephesians—As you catch a new vision of the church's exalted place in Christ in the heavenlies, I pray that you may be filled with all the fulness of God and walk worthy of your high vocation.

Philippians—I thank you for your material gift and pray that you advance spiritually and rejoice in the Lord despite all difficulties.

Colossians—Beware lest philosophers keep you from giving

Christ preeminence as Head of the body the church.

1 Thessalonians—I'm sending Timothy to strengthen you in your afflictions and to give further instructions about the coming of the Lord.

2 Thessalonians—Don't be upset by that false report saying that the day of the Lord has already come. The lawless one must first be revealed. May you be established in every good work and word.

1 Timothy—Remain at Ephesus to teach, urge faithfulness to sound doctrine and godliness, and prescribe the duties of the various classes of people.

2 Timothy—Do your best to come to me soon. Meanwhile don't be ashamed of the Lord or of me, but continue faithfully to teach and to preach the Word.

Titus—With full authority put the organization of the churches in working order and exhort to good deeds.

Philemon—I am sending Onesimus back to you. Receive him as you would receive me. If he owes you anything, charge it to my account.

Of the longer epistles Romans is largely doctrinal, while 1 and 2 Corinthians are mainly experiential. Romans stands in a class by itself, for it is formal, studiously structured with logical precision and skill, rising to heights of eloquence. The need in the church at Rome was a systematic intellectual argument that would satisfy the mind, a reasoned explanation for the crucial truth that justification before God rests not in the keeping of the law but in the merit of Christ's death for sin. Yet the Book of Romans has very personal sections: chapters 6—8, 12—16.

The other epistles are mainly experiential, with a few chapters predominantly doctrinal: 1 Corinthians 9, 2 Corinthians 3, 10—12, Galatians 1—4, Ephesians 2 and parts of 1 and 3, Colossians 1.

In the epistles of Paul we find the same balance and interweaving of inner and outer factors as we did in the gospel records. The approach to eternal truth is usually in terms of current needs and problems. No doubt the churches to whom Paul wrote read what he had written with great eagerness because it was beamed specifically to them. Each paragraph throbbed with his deep longing for their progress, whatever that next step might be, and for the defeat of Satan no matter how he then disguised himself.

So personal are Paul's letters that we can almost hear him answering the questions and comments of his readers as he writes. In Romans 9—11 he stops his argument to answer their questions about the salvation of the nation Israel in relation to the Gentiles. In 1 Corinthians 15:35 he says, "But some one will ask, 'How are the dead raised?' " After he has said firmly to timid young Timothy, "These things command and teach," he adds to encourage him, "Let no man despise thy youth" (1 Timothy 4:11, 12).

We observe also that Paul expects insight and understanding of the truth of God to issue in action upon that truth. Paul expects spiritual life to flow from vision and appropriation: vision of Christ's full provision for our salvation, of His exaltation as our great High Priest; appropriation of the believer's riches in Christ, of the power of the indwelling Spirit. He expects exemplary Christian walk to accompany clear understanding of the truth.

Yet Paul doesn't assume that right doctrine will automatically result in right living. He doesn't exclude the subject of Christian living from any of the letters. How often he exhorts his readers to be not conformed to this world, to do all to the glory of God, to walk worthy of the high vocation, to abound more and more in love, to teach sound doctrine! In most of the epistles the doctrinal concepts are interwoven with the personal messages, though in some cases the two elements are rather distinct.

Emphasis on the Christian's inner life is also balanced with its outward manifestation. While Ephesians and Colossians stress the exaltation of the body of Christ along with its preeminent Head, the pastorals (1 Timothy,

2 Timothy, Titus) show how this body functions in its organization on earth. The last half of Ephesians and Colossians come down from glorious heights to the very practical relations of wives and husbands, children and parents, servants and masters. In 1 Corinthians the Apostle answers real needs as well as felt needs; in the midst of his discussion of the problems of disorder at the Lord's table and confusion in the use of tongues, he writes the exquisite poem on the nature of Christian love.

Paul continually motivates his readers to accept the authority of the Holy Scriptures and of himself as God's chosen mouthpiece. In his mind there is never the slightest doubt about the sanction of either of these. But his readers need to be continually urged to sharpen their response to the Word of God. In stimulating the Philippians to make Christ the very center of their lives, he uses the example of Christ, of other men, and seven times the example of his own life. He also shows that God is at work in them, that the peace of God will be theirs, that they are lights shining in a perverse world, that he wants to be proud of them, that he wants them to obtain credit from the Lord. Each motivation is designed to make a strong inner reaction that will result in radiant outer lives.

In closing his epistles, Paul often adds greetings or warnings to individuals. Sometimes these personal references are quite extensive, as in Romans 16, 1 Corinthians 14, Colossians 4, 2 Timothy 4. All these people's names have been incorporated in the written canon of Scripture because Paul had personal words for them! How thrilling for those who are commended! How distressing for those who need reprimand! How touching to read in 2 Timothy 4:13, "When you come, bring the cloak that I left . . . at Troas, also the books, and above all the parchments."

Thus it is clear from a study of the Old Testament wilderness school and the sermons and epistles of the Apostle Paul that what we found in the gospels is corroborated by the rest of Scripture. In His infinite wisdom the Lord begins His lessons where people are, with their needs and problems, He helps them to gain insight and understanding of eternal truth that answers their problems, and then to relate that truth to everyday living.

V

THE USE OF THE BIBLE
IN TEACHING

"The Bible! Indeed, not an ordinary Book! Hated and hounded as no other book has ever been, and yet indestructible; despised, and yet honored; derided, and yet highly esteemed; declared dead, and yet alive. Mighty emperors and kings and priests have shunned no toil and no guilt in order to exterminate it; wise and scholarly men have, in the sweat of their brow, thoroughly refuted it; and now, that higher criticism lords over it and science has done away with it, it is spreading over the whole earth with astonishing rapidity in millions of copies and hundreds of languages, and is being read and preached from pole to pole; and, in the faith and power of the Word, Negroes submit to being burned alive, and Armenians and Chinese to being tortured to death. Ho, all ye scholars and critics! do but write such a book, and we will believe you!

"Complete in itself—'accursed any man that shall add

unto or take away'—unchanged and unchangeable, this Bible stands for centuries, unconcerned about the praise and the reproach of men; it does not accommodate itself to progress, does not recant a single word, remains grandly simple and divinely overpowering, and in its sight all men are equal and feel their impotency.

"With sublime freedom it strides through the history of mankind, dismisses entire nations with a glance, with a word, in order to tarry a long time with the deeds of a shepherd. . . . Of this Book thousands of the best and most talented among men have testified, not only that they never tired of reading and studying it, but also that it constantly grew grander, richer, more unfathomable. How often some unseeming word, that you have read a hundred times, suddenly opens up, revealing its deep, hidden meaning! . . . Through the whole the Great Designer weaves the glorious drama of redemption, in which frail creatures of the dust are raised to heavenly places through no merit of their own.

"In the beginning of His Word, God steps forth out of His eternity, grand and resplendent, the ground, principle, and cause of the universe, the Creator of creation, He, who, in incomprehensible omnipotence, creates, and there is no one who could say, Why doest thou thus? At the close of His Word, where a new eternal creation begins, heavenly creatures and powers cast their crowns at His feet, crying: 'Thou art worthy, O Lord, to receive glory and honor and power: for Thou hast created all things, and for Thy pleasure they are and were created.' 'Alleluia: for the Lord God omnipotent reigneth!' "[7]

We evangelicals concur wholeheartedly on the *place* of the Bible in teaching, but we have given little thought to the *use* of the Bible. We have staunchly defended the verbal inspiration of the Scriptures and the infallibility of our authority against those who would judge the Word of God rather than letting it judge them. We hold that God has revealed Himself objectively in the propositions of Scripture, as well as in its history and narratives and poetry. Our subjective experience of Christ stems from the doctrines of the Word. We hold that "faith cometh by hearing, and hearing by the word of God" (Romans 10:17).

The strength of the evangelical position has been the retention of this high view of Scripture. We have taught it as truth to the exclusion of the opinions of men, we have tried to understand it and faithfully to convey its meaning. We believe that it is the Word of God that does the work of God by the Spirit of God and the Christian teacher. We very readily quote 2 Timothy 3:16, 17, but we don't always obey these verses. "All scripture is given by inspiration of God, and is profitable for doctrine, for reproof, for correction, for instruction in righteousness: That the man of God may be perfect, thoroughly furnished unto all good works." In addition to doctrine, Scripture is to be used to reprove and correct daily living, to train, nurture, discipline in holiness in order that the believer may be mature at each stage of his development, expressing the Christ-life by all the good works that are appropriate for his age level.

Instead of nurturing toward maturity, we often play Bible baseball with our classes on Sunday morning. We try to warm them up by throwing Bible words at them and asking them to toss them back to us. When the game begins, we pitch factual questions at them. But when they go home and take off their "Sunday togs," they're the same people underneath. They haven't experienced the presence of the Lord. They haven't met Him. We haven't been changing life. We've merely been playing at the game of life. We've repeated words and repeated words. We've insisted that our pupils repeat words. We seldom fathom the depth of ignorance and unreality "over which we skate on a film of words." When unreal words are added to unreal words, the whole process is founded upon unreality. When our young people crack the thin ice of words on which they've been skating, they plunge into the cold water below and are usually lost to the class and to the gospel.

There are enough facts abroad in our day to convert the

world if all of us acted on the truth that we mentally under-stand and accept. But the Bible as we have taught it hasn't proved to be the dynamite that we expected. What kind of class would your class be if each member obeyed the Scrip-ture that he understands? What kind of church would your church be if each member lived what he professes? The Lord holds us responsible to live up to the light that we have. The Bible always connects doctrine with practice.

Most of our pupils are not memorizing Scripture the way we'd like them to because they see no need to do so. They are not searching the Scriptures because they don't see what difference it will make in their own lives, they don't see the relevance of doctrine to life. They have seldom met the Living Word through the written Word, and so do not pick up the Book with the eager expectation of having dealings with the Lord of glory. They have never been guided in finding personal spiritual nourishment that is more vitalizing than physical food and drink.

Therefore our main problems in the use of Scripture are to get through the written Word to the Living Word, and to translate doctrine into life.

It is not enough to know about the Lord; we must *know* Him.

It is not enough to believe our beliefs; we must *believe* Him.

It is not enough to take the Word as God's; we must *take God at His Word.*

ESSENTIAL MEANS TO THE END

The focus in teaching is for the pupil to hear God speak a personal word to him and for him to respond personally. The Lord always takes the initiative, in love revealing Him-self and His will. We teachers work with Him to get the pupil ready to listen in the context of his daily life, which is the only situation that has meaning for him. Revelation demands response. God says, "I have made all this provision for you; I expect this of you in return." He wants to set up personal relationships with each pupil, ever more intimate. Christianity is Person-to-person.

Have you ever pondered the question: What is the greatest thing in life? Is it not relationships—first with the Center of the universe, then feeling right about ourselves, then reaching out to others? After we get back in tune with our Maker, and feel comfortable about ourselves, we are free to relate to others. Our goal in life is satisfying relationships.

But often we get sidetracked onto goals of lesser value. We mistake means for ends. In Bible teaching we get absorbed with words and programs and methods. The Holy Spirit is the model Teacher, who does not speak on His own, but takes the things of Christ and shows them to us (John 16:14). Because evangelicals have such a high view of Scripture, we sometimes get our pupils related to the written Word without getting them through to the Living Word. We strive to get them to understand doctrines, memorize, complete their workbooks without dealing personally with the Living Lord. Words, doctrines, ideas are stepping-stones to the Person of the Lord—essential means to spiritual reality.

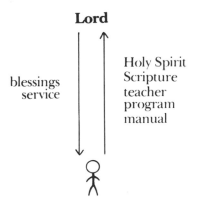

The Bible itself employs very graphic symbols to illustrate the way in which it is to be used. It speaks of itself as:

> seed to produce fruit—Luke 8:11
> rain and snow to refresh—Isaiah 55:10–11
> food to nourish—Jeremiah 15:16
> milk and meat—Hebrews 5:12–14
> honey and gold—Psalms 19:10
> lamp to illumine—Psalms 119:105
> mirror to reflect—James 1:22–24
> laver to cleanse—Psalms 119:9
> sword to pierce, critic to discern—Hebrews 4:12
> fire to consume, hammer to break—Jeremiah 23:29.

These figures are not ends in themselves, but means to the end of promoting interaction with the Lord of life.

Like a seed the Word is insignificant in outward appearance—merely one Book among millions of others, yet containing life-giving potential encased within a hard shell—words and sentences that can be printed in letters on pages and even repeated without meaning. But when that hard outer shell is broken by soft, warm, receptive surroundings, the enormous potential is released to produce all kinds of fruit. Seeds exist for one purpose, to produce fruit. The seed of the Word in the life of believers ought to multiply throughout the earth, to bring forth after its kind, to keep reproducing the Christ-life.

Scripture also serves as spiritual food, water, and light—essentials for daily nurture, training, and discipline; or in other words, the "instruction in righteousness" of 2 Timothy 3:16. No matter how beautiful and expensive a banquet board may be, it is never prepared for purposes of display only, merely to be admired for itself, but to be consumed, to be chewed and digested for the strengthening of living tissue. Food does not build life unless it is inwardly assimilated into the very flesh and blood of the eater. In His Word and through His Word God has provided a table richly spread for those who hunger and thirst after righteousness. When they rise from the table, He holds out to them a lamp for their feet as they walk the daily path.

For the reproof and correction of 2 Timothy 3:16, God provides a mirror to reflect our true state, to reveal how far short we fall of what we might be in Christ so that we will feel the need of cleansing in the laver where "the blood of Jesus Christ, his Son cleanseth us from all sin" (1 John 1:7). But it's not easy for the human soul, born in sin, to see himself as God sees him. The Word must often be a sharp two-edged sword cutting deep even to hidden motives and intentions that are never consciously countenanced, but which nevertheless are the determinants of action. As the sword of the Spirit, the Word should be an active agent in the spiritual warfare, yet how often this sharp instrument is worn dull by constant crude handling! The Word of God was not given merely to be repeated back, but to build spiritual life, to consume the old self-life and to break in pieces the stubborn will which will not give Christ first place.

Programs also may become ends in themselves rather than means to the end of drawing people to Christ. We may feel satisfied with our efforts if we put on attractive, forceful programs. We want our pupils to love us as teachers, but through us to love the Lord. Manuals serve their purpose when they lead in the direction of behavioral aims.

Sometimes the Lord must even withhold blessings that He would like to give because we would make them ends in themselves. We get involved with the good things He gives and forget the Giver. We even get so wrapped up in service that we're doing it in ourselves for ourselves.

THE EXAMPLE OF ISAIAH 55

Sometimes God's people, with the best of intentions, protest, "But you're making teaching too complicated. God tells us only to give out the Word. His Spirit will do the rest. He promises that His Word will not return unto Him void."

We are eternally grateful for the wonderful promise of Isaiah 55:11, but we must take it in its context. Before you read any comments on this outstanding chapter, won't you take time to study for yourself the following questions? This passage will mean more to you if you discover its basic principles for yourself.

What great promise does the Lord give in verse 11?

What is the context of this promise?

Why do ten verses lead up to this climactic statement in verse 11?

How many imperatives can you count in the first ten verses?

What is the significance of these imperatives?

In verses 12 and 13 what are said to be the results of the working of the Word?

What is the lesson pattern of this chapter of Scripture?

Verse 11 does not even begin a sentence; it finishes the comparison begun in verse 10. And verse 10 is one of four verses beginning with the conjunction "for." To find the significance of that little word we have to go back to the first verses, which give the main clauses of the chapter. When we observe sharply the structure of the first half of the chapter, we notice that a striking effect is gained by the use of one imperative after another: come, come, buy, eat, come, buy, hearken, eat, delight yourself, incline your ear, come, hear, seek the Lord, call upon Him. This lesson plan doesn't begin with Scripture, but with the pupil. He is first motivated and prepared for the truth. The imperatives show him his need of the Lord and His Word. Why aren't man's own ways sufficient? *For* God's ways are not his ways, *for* God's ways are infinitely higher than his ways, *for* His Word will provide what he basically needs, *for* God will produce joy and peace.

In summary we may say that verse 11 does not promise that under all circumstances the Word will accomplish God's purpose whenever it is spoken. The burden of the first half of the chapter is getting people who need the Lord to *feel* their need, to seek the Lord so that He can answer them. Isn't that also a problem that we face in our teaching? When people are hungry and thirsty for the Word of truth, they eagerly drink it in. But most people are smugly satisfied with their own selfish ways; they do not seek God's higher ways. He says, "Ask, and it shall be given you; seek, and ye shall find; knock, and it shall be opened unto you" (Matthew 7:7).

The comparison that is used in verse 10 is very enlightening. God's Word is like the rain and snow that come down from heaven. These elements do not return to the sky in the same form in which they came down, or they would fail to accomplish their purpose. God sends them to water the earth, to make it bring forth and bud, to give seed to the sower and bread to the eater. So He sends forth His Word, not to return to Him in the same form in which He gave it, but to refresh the earth spiritually, to provide daily spiritual revival and power. When God's Word is used to do this, God's people will go forth in joy and peace. Instead of thorns and briars that obstruct spiritual progress, will come up the cypress and myrtle for the benefit of mankind. Using God's Word as He intended will produce the fruits of righteousness that we all long to see.

Quite the contrary is sometimes the case, as in the following experience:

I can still remember so well my childhood Sunday school days when my teacher would tell me that I had learned a Scripture verse if I could quote it from memory. In our class we often had

Scripture memory contests, so I memorized verses by the dozen and usually won the first prize. Several years have passed since those days; I really can't remember many of those verses—in fact, I couldn't quote ten of them now. Did I really learn them?

Most of the verses contained words that were unfamiliar to me and the teacher never took time to explain what they meant. The verses were just so many words and phrases that I crammed into my head, but they never reached my heart. Consequently they never really affected my life except to make me feel proud because I had won the contest. (Ronald Wiebe)

CHRIST'S USE OF SCRIPTURE

The Son of God was the Master Teacher not only because He was one with the Father, because He knew what was in man, but also because the Word of God permeated His whole being. His use of it was both direct and indirect, formal and informal. He used material from all the divisions of the Old Testament. He often wove it into His personal conversation with individuals as well as into His discourses to crowds. He held men responsible for knowing and doing the will of God.

Scripture was so much a part of His being that He used it for many purposes by many methods. He used it to defeat Satan, to reveal who He was, to give authority for His words and deeds, to show the fulfillment of prophecy, to stimulate thinking and questioning, to answer questions, to instruct in righteousness, to correct wrong concepts and practices. He was continually showing the relation of the Old Testament to the matter at hand. He summed up all the Old Testament commandments in two that require love rather than knowledge, though of course love based on knowledge.

The sin of the Pharisees was that, while they knew the letter of the law, they failed to catch its essential spirit, to relate it to their inner life. While they knew the words of Scripture, they did not know Him of whom the Scripture spoke. Their knowledge of words made them proud and smug, but failed to accomplish the purpose for which it was given. When they rebuked Christ for eating with sinners, He told them to go and learn what God meant when He said in Hosea 6:6, "I desired mercy, and not sacrifice." He was answering in effect, "You are able to repeat the words of scripture like Hosea 6:6, but in understanding and practice you have no idea what the words imply."

To a larger group of Jews He said, "You search the scriptures, because you think that in them you have eternal life; and it is they that bear witness to me; yet you refuse to come to me that you may have life" (John 5:39,40 RSV). They had not heard the voice of God speaking through the words (John 5:37). To the Jews who had believed in Him the Lord said, "If ye continue in my word, then are ye my disciples indeed; And ye shall know [by experience as well as by conviction] the truth, and the truth shall make you free" (John 8:31,32). It takes more than God's Word in the mouth to insure God's power in the life.

A clear example of the method of Christ is found in Luke 4:16–30 when He read Scripture in the synagogue at Nazareth. He entered the synagogue as was His custom on the Sabbath day and stood up to read. The book of the prophet Isaiah was given to Him. He selected a particular passage; He did not begin at the beginning of the book nor follow what had been read previously, but selected exactly the part that His hearers needed, those with whom He had grown up, who were the hardest to convince who He was. He chose a passage that used the first person singular pronoun, that distinctly described His ministry without a word of explanation. The audience may have expected routine reading of Scripture, but so personal and effective was that reading that when He sat down, the eyes of all in the synagogue were fastened on Him. They wondered how these words of grace could come from a man they had always considered to be Joseph's son. Something happened when He read Scripture.

Then He took arguments right out of their own minds

and answered them by two forceful illustrations from Scripture. Though there were many widows in Israel at the time of Elijah's drought, he was sent out of his own country to a widow in Sidon; and Elisha healed the Syrian of leprosy, not his own countrymen who had the dread disease. So forceful were these illustrations that the congregation rose up in wrath and attempted to throw Him over the hill!

When the Word of God is brought to bear upon current needs, it produces action as it is meant to do, not always positive, but it changes things. People ought not to be able to listen to the Word of God without being changed. They are forming disastrous habits if they're ever allowed to do so.

THEORY OR LIFE?

In the gospel records two Greek words are translated by the English word "know." Merrill Tenney says in *The Genius of the Gospels:*

"Knowledge" in John represents both conviction and experience. The uses of the two words for "know" in the Gospel, *ginosko* and *oida,* suggest that the former means a knowledge derived from experiential contact, while the latter is a conviction produced by intuitive understanding. Not all exegetes agree on this point; but the fact remains that *ginosko* is used in passages where experiential rather than theoretical knowledge is implied, whereas the reverse is not true. The occurrence of this word in John 17:3 shows that experiential knowledge has a place in theological thinking; and that theoretical theology has the building of spiritual experience for its objective. Without the norm the experience cannot be tested; and without the experience the norm is only theory. John shows how both can be united in sound Christian faith. Theology must be practical to be effective, and creeds, to endure beyond the generation of their makers, must be vital as well as logical.[8]

The New Testament epistles sometimes use an even stronger word than *gnosis* to express the idea of knowledge, *epignosis,* full knowledge gained by experience. Kenneth Wuest says of Philippians 1:9:

> The full knowledge which these Philippians needed to gain by experience was a better understanding of God's Word as translated into their experience, and a clearer vision of the Lord Jesus in all the beauty and fragrance of His Person. A Christian can have an "understanding" knowledge of the Word, that is, be able to explain its meaning to others, without having an experiential knowledge of the same. But when that Christian has put the Word of God into practice in his life, then he has what Paul is talking about here.[9]

In Philippians 1:9 Paul prays that the love of these believers may abound yet more and more in experiential knowledge and spiritual discernment. We need to know a person before we love Him. We Christians must know *whom* we have believed as well as *what* we have believed (2 Timothy 1:12). The aim of all our Christian teaching is expressed in Ephesians 4:13, "Till we all come in the unity of the faith, and of the [experiential] knowledge of the Son of God, unto a perfect man, unto the measure of the stature of the fulness of Christ."

That ideal is high, very high. Of course it is high. As high as the heavens are high above the earth are God's ways above our ways. They are possible only for those who have entered into fulness of life, who are passionately devoted to the Lord because they have full experiential knowledge of Him, the power of His resurrection, the fellowship of His sufferings (Philippians 3:10).

In the words of Raymond Calkins, "Christianity has not been tried and found wanting; it has been found difficult and left untried."

The Bible knows no such thing as truth that is merely theoretical; in the Bible the truth is linked to the deed. We see this principle in its highest expression in the atonement. As theory alone, the atonement, profoundly true though it is, could never save a single soul. For the atonement to have saving efficacy, He who is the truth had to "do" it in His redemptive work on Calvary. Likewise with the whole of Scripture truth; it must be related to life to be known for what it really is.[10]

What a crime is anything that dulls the poignancy of the atonement, that allows the cross to seem commonplace, that keeps our emotions from leaping up at the very thought of the event that crowns the history of the race!

Andrew Murray, throughout his classic, *The Spirit of Christ,* keeps repeating the fact that the Scriptures are meant for the life as well as for the understanding. Higher and deeper than all thought, they enter into the very core of personality, where the Spirit of God has access. "Spiritual knowledge is not deep thought, but living contact, entering into and being united to the truth as it is in Jesus, a spiritual reality, a substantial substance."[11]

It is only the Living Presence that makes the Living Word; so the Kingdom comes not in word only, but in power. It is on this account that there is so much reading and preaching of the word that bears so little fruit; so much straining and praying for faith, with so little result. Men deal with the word more than with the Living God. Faith has very truly been defined as "Taking God at His word." With many this has only meant, Taking the word as God's; they did not see the force of the thought, *Taking God* at His word. A key or a door handle has no value until I use it for the lock and the door I want to open; it is alone in direct and living contact with God Himself that the word can work effectually and open the heart for God. Faith *takes God* at His word; it can only do this when and as He gives Himself. I may have in God's book all His precious promises most clear and full; I may have learnt perfectly to understand how I have but to trust the promise to have it fulfilled; and yet utterly fail to find the longed-for blessing. The faith that enters on the inheritance is the attitude of soul which waits for *God Himself,* first to speak His word to me, and then to do the thing He hath spoken.[12]

Murray reminds us that in the Garden of Eden two ways were set before Adam and Eve for attaining the likeness of God, two ways typified by the two trees, the tree of life, and the tree of the knowledge of good and evil. God's way was that through life would come the knowledge and likeness of God. But Satan assured Adam that it was through knowledge that man may be like the Most High.[13] Ever since then it has been difficult for men to put knowledge in its rightful place.

Many people today know a great deal about the Lord Jesus without knowing Him. They call Him "Lord, Lord," they throng the places of worship, they may be busily engaged in "His work." All our knowledge, understanding, and doctrine ought to help us to know Christ better, for He is spiritual reality. All our methods should help us to get through to reality, to Him, never be substitutes for Him or hindrances in getting to Him. In all things Christ should have the preeminence (Colossians 1:18).

A middle-aged adult describes her first Sunday at Sunday school in a new town:

It was hard for me to get ready to go to church on that first Sunday, but I felt that I needed to have a few minutes of peace and quiet away from home. It had been so nice back in Allentown to settle down and think my own thoughts on Sunday morning as the teacher of my class droned on and on. He usually taught prophecy, for that was his particular interest in the Bible, and since I understood prophecy, I didn't need to give close attention. I can remember only a few times when I bothered to speak up, like the time when the teacher said that Jesus Himself was going to rule in the earthly Jerusalem. Then I told him he was wrong, for I had heard an evangelist say that Jesus would rule in the heavenly Jerusalem.

From the minute I entered the door of this new church, I could see that this Sunday school wasn't like my old one. The people seemed to be plotting against my settling down in peace and quiet. They were almost too friendly; they asked me all about myself. They all had Bibles and insisted that I use one too—even had extras for newcomers like me.

I began to wonder who the teacher was and if we were going to have a Bible lesson, for a man introduced as Mr. Baker asked the class to pray for his son who had recently been keeping bad company. Then the man who turned out to be the teacher of the class asked us to pray also about a young girl who had run away to the city. It was such a personal prayer time that I could hardly keep back the tears as I thought of my own sister's trouble with her daughter.

After prayer, one of the women commented upon the fickleness and cocky know-it-all attitude of the young people of our day. The teacher then asked what were the differences between young people and adults. The members of the class could tell the differences, all right. We were pretty sure of ourselves until the teacher asked if all adults had discarded the fickleness and cockiness of youth. We began to think of adults who hadn't, until one man remarked, "I wonder how many of us here in this class have really left behind the childish selfishness of young people."

Then the teacher really stepped in. He suggested that we turn to the day's lesson on the change that took place in the Apostle Peter as he gradually grew from immaturity to maturity. First we looked up passages that described how he acted when Christ called him from his fishing.

When we began to use our Bibles, I was embarrassed. For the others turned immediately to the right book and the right verse, but I was still shuffling pages when they began to discuss Peter. And the members of the class did as much talking as the teacher! They seemed to enjoy it, and sometimes got away from the subject. But the teacher kept them on the track and was ready with the next place to read. He also asked some searching questions that hit me between the eyes. I felt as guilty as I had felt last night when the cop caught me after I'd driven through a red light in my hurry to get home.

But the other men and women didn't seem to be uncomfortable when the teacher implied that we, today, ought to be like Peter—even the Apostle Peter! I never saw people so ready to talk and to tell what the Bible said to them. They didn't just read the Bible; they applied everything to themselves.

When the teacher asked me if I wouldn't like to read a couple of verses, I could hardly get the words out. I guess they thought I'd never read the Bible before. Certainly I've never been in a class like this one.

At the end of the hour we prayed again. How we prayed! I guess I haven't prayed like that since I was saved. Those people were asking the Lord so earnestly to change them that I could feel myself being changed. I surely hadn't realized before how far I was from being "a real adult," and how much the Lord expected of me.

At the dinner table that noon my husband (who never goes to church) wanted to know what had happened to me. You see, on Sunday noon I usually talked over all the people I'd seen at church and all the gossip I'd heard. Now I told him about Peter, and how the Lord changed him from a childish weakling to a mature adult.

But the greatest blessing from the Sunday school class came that evening, after my husband and I had enjoyed the afternoon at home. I guess this was the first Sunday afternoon in a long time that I hadn't worked on him to take me some place away from the house. He said, "I can't imagine what happened to my nagging wife today. Maybe I better go to this new church to see what kinda religion they got there."

CENTRALITY OF THE PERSON OF CHRIST

2 Peter 1:3–8 describes the process of Christian maturity. It begins with an announcement so tremendous that it is hard to take it at face value. God's divine power has granted to us ALL THINGS that make for vital life and godliness. All things! Already granted! Ours for the taking! How? Through the true knowledge of Himself. Not just facts about, but full knowledge, personal, intimate, experiential. The Maker of heaven and earth wants us to know Him as a person, the Person He truly is. When we see who He is —His glory, excellence, splendor, might, in contrast with the corruption around us through evil desires, we want His quality of life, to exchange our frustrations for His fulfillment.

How do we do this? We dare the risk of faith and step out on His promises, which we find to be precious indeed, magnificent, great beyond all price. He waits for us to appropriate what He has already granted. In the process of walking with Him, we become partakers of the divine nature, share in the very being of God, and our very nature is changed. "We all with open face beholding as in a mirror the glory of the Lord are being changed into His likeness from one degree of glory to another (this glory refers to us!) for this comes from the Lord the Spirit (2 Corinthians 3:18).

Are we afraid of such glorious thoughts? Some Christians who have received forgiveness of sin haven't received much else of all that is waiting for them. It is hard to take time to gaze at the Majesty as we rush about in our push-button society.

The Lord can't give His power to weaklings who would

use it to destroy, but to those who are ready to press toward the mark of the high calling of maturity in Christ. Leaving behind anything that weakens, Peter says: apply all diligence, do your level best, make every effort, try your hardest to develop balanced maturity. Supplement your faith with

> virtue, which is moral maturity,
> knowledge, which is intellectual maturity,
> self-control, which is physical maturity,
> fortitude, which is emotional maturity,
> piety, which is spiritual maturity,
> brotherly kindness, which is social maturity.

And top it off with love, which binds the whole together—love, the sign of discipleship, the greatest eternal quality. While faith makes all things possible, love makes all joyous.

Since the Lord made us as complex as we are, He realistically meets the needs of all aspects of our beings. It's a shame when one immature aspect of personality keeps a Christian from fully using many strong qualities. He can keep us well-rounded and balanced, for He has planted in us the seed of the new nature, the very life of the Eternal, which is our responsibility to cultivate.

But these are such high standards for character that none of us has arrived, none of us has attained them. Why don't we become discouraged? Peter says, if these qualities are yours and are increasing, if you are making steady progress, you can take courage.

Then we can be effective and fruitful, not in service, as we might expect Peter to say, but again, in the knowledge of our Lord Jesus Christ. Our knowledge of the Lord is both means and end to fulness of life. God's ultimate intention is to make many sons like Himself. Service is the natural overflow, but emphasis on service can be an obstacle to fulness of life. The emphasis in Christian teaching is on the Person of Christ. He is the WHAT, He is the HOW, He is the WHY.

WORSHIP BASED ON INSTRUCTION

A secular lesson is finished when pupils apply the instruction that has been taught, but not Christian education. After we catch a vision of the Lord of Lords, who condescends to enter our world to have personal dealings with human creatures, the natural result is worship of the high and holy One. Worship is the culmination of spiritual experience in which self reaches out for God, feels Him near, and adores Him. We enter His presence not to keep learning, but to meet His person, our Creator-Redeemer. We bow before Him, who is worthy of all praise, and adjust our will to His. Jesus told the Samaritan woman that He *seeks* worship in spirit and in truth. We can never earn or repay what He has done for us, but we can worship with all that is in us.

To complete the process that instruction began, we praise God for the particular attributes that were brought out in the preceding instruction. Again, as emphasized earlier in this chapter, Biblical facts are the means to the end of preparing for this highest spiritual activity, for in worship we get through the written Word to the Living Word. It is the Person of God Himself who satisfies our deepest longings, whose presence fills us with His fulness. While Bible study informs the mind, worship challenges will and emotions.

Worship materials are chosen to continue the same aim and theme as the Bible lesson. The difficulty is to use ideas and words that express what the pupils are experiencing inside. At the beginning we need songs that are directed personally to the Lord, praising Him for His love or faithfulness or whatever the content focused. The Scripture selected is often a Psalm of praise. At the end of a service we can challenge each other to obey the Lord's commands, as "Who Is on the Lord's Side?" We continually ask ourselves, "Can the pupils truly mean all the words we ask them to sing, especially those worded in the first person?"

If worship precedes instruction, it is usually so general that it becomes routine, which can be deadly. Isaiah (29:13) and Jesus (Matthew 15:8) both warned against honoring God with our lips while our hearts are far from Him. To keep any element of worship from being merely routine, infinite creative variations are possible in building to a climax of prayer, the closest approach to God, when decisions are made and commitments renewed.

VI

THE TEACHING-LEARNING
PROCESS

After discovering the Scriptural foundations for Christian teaching, we come to the practical question of "How." How can we help pupils to get through the written Word to the Living Word? How can we help them translate Scripture into life? How can we help them take the next step toward maturity in Christ? Even in asking these questions, we see that the pupils must have a large place in the process, for it is they who must have dealings with the Lord; they must change their daily conduct, they must grow in grace. Our problem is to bring them to Christ, help them grow in Christ, and send them out for Christ. We can't receive Christ for them. We can't learn for them. According to the old adage, "You can lead a horse to water, but you can't make him drink." What is teaching but helping people to learn? Therefore the basic problem is not teaching, but learning. Unless we discover how people learn, we won't be able to teach as we ought.

TRANSFERRING THE LEARNING PROCESS FROM TEACHER TO PUPIL

It is true that pupils are always learning something, but often what they learn is not what the teacher intended to teach. While a lackluster teacher talks on and on, they may be deciding that they'll leave Sunday school just as soon as their parents stop forcing them to come. While a scholarly teacher strings generalization after generalization, they may be learning that the Bible is a very dull book. While an unprepared teacher rambles on in prayer, they may be learning that prayer time is the moment for carrying out their own ingenious devices.

A pupil's growth is determined not by what he hears, but by what he does about what he hears. The important thing is what is happening inside the pupil. He may accept or he may reject whatever is going on outside. Learning is what the pupil does and what outer forces do to him. We teachers can influence these inner factors only by manipulating the outer. If we work with the Spirit of God, He can use us to effect inner changes.

Modern man cannot hope to improve upon the concept of teaching that the Lord God Himself has given in John 16:13. Because the Holy Spirit is the only Teacher who is able to work both inside and outside the pupil, Christ told His disciples that the Spirit would guide them into all the truth and declare to them the things that are to come. Teaching then is guiding and declaring, guiding pupils and declaring truth. A real teacher does not hesitate to declare truth in a context of guidance. But if he only declares, he becomes a preacher. A teacher must be skilled in guiding, directing, helping pupils in their learning.

Teaching may be compared to conducting a guided tour. The tourists have decided whether they wish to see Europe, South America, or the Holy Land. The competent guide is one who has previously taken the trip, usually many times, and who is familiar with all the points of interest, so that he can help the group map out their itinerary and answer their questions. He facilitates the trip by making necessary arrangements and leads them to the main attractions so that every hour brings new experiences. The satisfaction of the tourists comes from their firsthand experiences with new people and places. Can you imagine the manager of a tour saying to a group who wanted to sightsee, "Since I've already made this trip, you won't need to go. I'll tell you all about it"?

Yet that's what many of us teachers are doing. We have learned a great deal because we have enjoyed rich, new experiences with the Lord. In teaching we always learn more than our pupils because we get more involved in the process than they do. But instead of guiding them through the type of experiences that we have had, we try to short-cut the process by giving them only the end result of our experience. They don't want to know merely what happened to other people, not even to the people of the Bible; they want exciting new experiences to happen to them—firsthand, personally.

Of course the easiest way to teach is merely to tell. We can tell what we have to say without any regard for the pupils. It matters not if Jerry feels homesick with an aching void inside, if Alice is feeling spiteful because of what happened last Sunday, if Nancy is full of questions about what we're saying, if Alden has heard it many times before. But guide pupils? Guide them into firsthand experiences? Jerry and Alice and Nancy and Alden? How can we do that? That will take some doing. Yes, it will. But nothing else will suffice for the Christian teacher. Christ wants to teach in His own way through us today. As we found in Chapter III, what Christ does is determined by what His pupils do. We do not naturally teach according to the Word of God. Every area of life that God's revelation enters is changed, teaching being no exception.

Our big job as teachers is to set up a situation that is propitious for learning, in which Jerry and Alice and Nancy and Alden will want to find God's higher ways. We can make everything in the classroom situation favorable to learning rather than militating against it, as is often the case.

In the first place we'll project ourselves into the place of our pupils, and try to feel as they feel, think as they think, walk in their shoes. We'll put aside the fact that we know the lesson of the day, but remember only that they don't. We won't stay in our own world and try to call across a great gulf into theirs. We'll try to tap their world. We'll transfer the learning process from the teacher to the pupil. Then teaching becomes a great adventure with the Master Teacher Himself.

THE NATURE OF GROWTH

Scripture often speaks of spiritual growth in terms of physical growth: "Thy wife shall be as a fruitful vine by the sides of thine house: thy children like olive plants round about thy table" (Psalms 128:3); "Every plant, which my heavenly Father hath not planted, shall be rooted up" (Matthew 15:13).

We recall that Comenius also made extensive use of this analogy. While there are many instructive similarities between natural and supernatural growth, there is one great difference. The lower order of plant life has no will of its own; it merely follows the sequence marked out for it by its Maker according to its kind. The action of the human will is necessary in regeneration to receive God's gift of His Son. This decisive action has no parallel in nature. No matter what a person's training or mental understanding may be, we won't assume that he is a Christian until we observe unmistakable evidence of his being born from above. However, just as there is a period of prenatal development before physical birth, there is a period of prenatal development before spiritual birth, sometimes longer, sometimes shorter. Before regeneration, the young child's parents try to help him to say no to his own selfish ways and yes to the Lord's higher ways; yet strictly speaking, only after spiritual birth can the new creation in Christ be said to grow. Our concern is to see the individual making steady spiritual progress from physical birth to death.

Scripture's Analogy with Physical Growth

Although the human sapling may suddenly spurt ahead in his development when he makes right decisions, spiritual growth as well as natural growth is usually a gradual ongoing process. Just as in a cornfield we see "first the blade, then the ear, after that the full corn in the ear" (Mark 4:28), so we are to grow up into Christ in all things, for He is the head of the body the church (Ephesians 4:15). Under healthy conditions growth is steady and consistent. Though startling changes may not be seen day by day, progress should be evident. If reliance is placed on periodic revivals or contests, the result is likely to be a spurt followed by a decline, then another effort to rally, followed by relapse.

Growth takes place from within outward. "The righteous flourish like the palm tree, and grow like a cedar in Lebanon . . . They still bring forth fruit in old age, they are ever full of sap and green" (Psalms 92:12,14 RSV). The roots of the tree take nourishment from the soil up through the trunk, out through the branches to every last leaf and bud. Bud, blossom, and fruit are all an integral part of the very life of the tree.

How different the Christmas tree, that has been severed

from its source. For a few weeks we doll it up with lights and bright balls and tinsel. For a short time it is truly a spectacle, but soon it is thrown away. It was only meant to be decoration. But don't we teachers sometimes work for "Christmas tree" effects? We train our pupils to repeat verses that are only words to them or to say pretty little poems in special-day programs. These words may perhaps entertain adults, but what is happening inside the pupils as a result? Is the Word of God merely "hung on" the pupil for decoration, or is it being assimilated into his inner being? The Book of Proverbs admonishes us to keep our heart with all diligence, for out of it are the issues of life (Proverbs 4:23).

The issues of life for "every blooming thing" depend upon the nature of the soil, whether or not it has been prepared. "Behold, a sower went forth to sow," said Jesus, "and some seed fell by the wayside, some fell on stony ground, some fell among thorns, and other seed fell on good ground" (Matthew 13:3–8). In most of our Bible classes we have several kinds of soil represented. How can we expect to teach without knowing what kind of seed each pupil is ready to receive? When the eternal destiny of souls is at stake, how can we be content to take whatever seed is nearest at hand and scatter it broadside regardless of the soil? Some type of seed will grow in even the poorest soil if we care enough to find out what type that is.

Even the sturdiest of plants continually need sunshine, rain, and pruning. "The Lord God is a sun and shield" (Psalms 84:11); "He shall come down like rain upon the mown grass: as showers that water the earth" (Psalms 72:-6). Christ said, "Every branch in me that beareth not fruit he taketh away: and every branch that beareth fruit, he purgeth it, that it may bring forth more fruit" (John 15:2). Nourishment and exercise are needed every day of one's life, from birth to death. Some teachers relax their efforts after a soul has been born from above. What, leave a new-born spiritual babe to fend for himself when he needs constant care and feeding?

THE TEST OF REAL LEARNING

"By their fruits ye shall know them" (Matthew 7:20). The righteous man "shall be like a tree planted by the rivers of water, that bringeth forth his fruit in his season; his leaf also shall not wither; and whatsoever he doeth shall prosper" (Psalms 1:3).

What kind of fruit has been the result of our teaching? Have we been satisfied when our pupils have been able to recite Bible verses, repeat Bible facts, earn awards for perfect attendance? What aspects of our teaching have we been particularly concerned about? How smoothly we could tell a Bible story or give a lecture? How quiet our classroom is? What is the real test of our teaching, the test of real learning on the part of the pupils?

During the week when our pupils mingle with non-Christians, is it evident that the Word of God is operating in their lives? On the playground could a stranger pick them out as most unselfish, loyal, truthful, cooperative? In school or in the office are they most dependable? At home are they obedient, courteous, lovable? Do their families ask, "What have you been doing to my boy?" because his conduct is changing? When you aren't with them, do they manifest the fruit of the Spirit? (Galatians 5:22,23.)

In our own spiritual experience we find that when God gives us new truth He soon puts us to the test over it. The minute we refuse to act on His truth, that minute we begin to backslide. The minute we act on it we begin to pulsate with new life and to go on to spiritual victory.

One of the most haunting phrases in Scripture is "nothing but leaves" (Mark 11:12–14). When Jesus saw in the distance a fig tree in leaf, He went to see if He could find anything on it to assuage His hunger. He found nothing but leaves. May this phrase characterize the efforts of none of us! It is possible to go through all the motions of Bible teaching, to speak Bible words, sing hymns, pray, mark attendance books and prepare object lessons, without spiritual fruit. But if we do the Lord's work in the Lord's way, "in due season we shall reap, if we faint not" (Galatians 6:9).

Today when the Lord seeks in our churches for "the fruit of the travail of his soul" (Isaiah 53:11 RSV), is He satisfied with what He finds? Or does He find "nothing but leaves"? The fruit that He seeks is disciples, for He has commanded us to go and teach all nations, make learners of all nations, make disciples of all nations (Matthew 28:19). Disciples are Christians who can stand alone in Christ, who are multiplying themselves, who are dying to their old self-life, falling like a grain of wheat into the ground in order that they may reproduce themselves (John 12:24). Disciples are following Jesus, are daily walking with Him rather than continuing their old selfish ways.

But alongside disciples in our churches today are many converts. Yes, they've been saved, they once met Christ, they have eternal life. But like the fig tree that Jesus cursed, they are bearing no fruit. They are producing "nothing but leaves." They go to church, they sing gospel songs, they know the cardinal doctrines. But they are not multiplying themselves. They have turned around from dependence upon themselves to dependence upon the Lord for salvation, but they are not walking in the faith that saved them. The Lord never asked us to make converts.

Our methods of teaching are largely responsible for the number of converts who should be disciples. When our boys and girls have repeated Bible words, we have said that they have "learned" them, and perhaps have given them a star for it. That, to the children, was the end of the process. Therefore to say Bible words like "love one another" was to learn the verse. Is "love one another" an easy memory verse? When has a person learned to love others? Have *you* learned to love others? What is the real test of love for others? How *easy* to say three little words! How *hard* to show love to people who are unlovely, in circumstances that impel self-preservation!

How can we help converts to become disciples by practicing love? We can provide opportunities for practice as part of our program. Right in our classrooms we can set up situations for the practice of sharing, working together, being courteous, thinking of others, taking turns, denying self. Projects and parties planned during the Bible school hour but carried out during the week call for other kinds of Christian conduct. But the real test comes when the pupils leave the realm of our supervision and are on their own. If they actually show love in new situations at home, on the playground, in school, or in the office, they have truly learned to love one another. If not, they have failed to learn those Bible words.

INDIVIDUALITY IN GROWTH

If each leaf on a tree differs from any other, how much more the complex human personality, each with its unique combination of traits. Each of us has been fashioned by the great Designer to bear a special manifestation of His own Son. He needs every one of us in our own place to show forth His whole character. It may be natural for us to feel that some defect mars the symmetry of our makeup or the usefulness of our service, but we are exactly as He planned in His perfect knowledge and power.

Just as some seeds do best in light, sandy, well-drained soil, while others prefer rich heavy ground, human personality is even more sensitive to environing conditions. Some seeds need full sunshine, while others will grow in shade. Some will grow year after year in the same location, while others should be removed to another place. Some of our pupils need very tender, delicate treatment for they are sensitive and easily bruised. Some respond best to harsh shock treatment. Some are so eager that they grasp even the incidentals that are tossed in as extras. Some are so dull to spiritual things that the core of the truth must be approached from many angles before they catch a glimmer of its meaning. Each has his own rate of development, his own special needs.

How can we expect to make one lesson fit all the different individuals in our class? At every contact our aim is nothing less than to help each one take a step toward maturity in Christ. The first thing we'll do is to pray definitely for each one each day. What changes do we want to see in Jerry? Why does Jerry feel and think as he does? Can we clearly analyze why Jerry behaves as he does? Can we visualize the world as it looks from his back porch? If not, we'll find out these things. We'll visit his home, his schoolroom or his office, his gang, his recreation center. Then we'll be able intelligently to pray for him. Moreover, as we get the Lord's viewpoint on Jerry, we'll be ready to work with the Spirit in His own way to help Jerry.

LEARNING AS AN INNER PROCESS

Of course true learning has outward manifestations, yet they will not represent real and permanent changes unless something has first happened inside. The truth of God must progressively control the inner life.

If we are going to work with the Lord to change pupils inwardly, we must begin where the change is needed, with what already controls their behavior. What is it that prompts our actions? It is our needs, our strong innate drives, which the Almighty Himself has put within us. The concept of need is one of the key concepts of education. All mankind have physical needs, for the satisfaction of which we expend prodigious efforts, lie, steal, or go to war. We have emotional needs of security, affection, recognition, freedom from guilt, and new experiences. In advanced cultures where standards of living are high, these psychological needs motivate most of our actions. Mentally we all need activity along the lines of present interests, challenges to our current abilities, and broadening new intellectual experiences. Spiritually we need to be reconciled with our Creator-Redeemer, to mature in the privileges and responsibilities of life in Christ, to work creatively with Him in order to apprehend that for which we were apprehended of Christ.

Although many of these needs are concurrently present, whichever need is most basic and most pressing will claim our attention, our interest, our effort. Our whole being is consciously and unconsciously searching for the means of meeting these needs. If we see no relation between an event and our own needs, we pay no attention to it.

Why did the Creator constitute us with these needs? So that He could satisfy them with Himself. He is waiting to supply all our needs according to His riches in glory by Christ Jesus (Philippians 4:19). He wants to speak to us daily in the language that we know best, the circumstances of our everyday lives. Every problem in life ought to drive us to Him for its solution. Most of the lessons Christ taught in the gospels started with these personal needs. We as teachers help our pupils to see and appropriate the Lord as the answer to the personal needs that He has ordained.

When we bow before Christ as King of kings and Lord of lords, we find all our needs met in this one glorious Savior! As Christ delivers us from the power of sin in the form of the world, the flesh, and the devil, we become increasingly free to devote ourselves to Him. As we delight ourselves in Him and become identified with Him in His death and resurrection, He can take us up into His divine purposes and give us a spiritual burden that He will accomplish in us. As the self-life is denied, He becomes the center of all of life. Then our entire concentration is that we may know Him, and the power of His resurrection and the fellowship of His sufferings. We are no longer concerned about our own needs but about His great plan of redemption for the world.

Sometimes the needs that are felt most urgently by our pupils are inconsequential in the light of eternity. Yet we may be obliged to start with these "felt needs" in order to make a point of contact. Our purpose then will be to lead from these "felt needs" to real spiritual needs, just as Christ did when He led the Samaritan woman from physical water to spiritual water. He might never have had a hearing with her if He had started with living water and true worship. Starting with "felt needs" doesn't mean that we're stopping there.

Is starting a lesson with the pupils' interests the same as starting with a need? What is the distinction between an interest and a need? If we are teaching children the story of David and Goliath, we might begin with their interest in slingshots, which would probably enlist immediate attention. They would be glad to share their experiences with slings, they'd be able to project themselves into the story of David, and would listen especially for the part about the sling. After the story, what would most likely be their comments? "Wish I had a sling. How could I get one? I wouldn't need a giant to hit. I'd settle for a bird, or a man's hat. I want a sling." Is that the response we're seeking as the result of the story?

Contrast the approach to that lesson in terms of a personal need. Discuss with the children the things they know they ought to do but they find hard to do. "These are our giants, the things that may slay us if we aren't careful. David had his giant too, and he overcame his. How did he do it? Can we too be strong in the Lord and in the power of His might? How? This week?" Yes, a need pierces deep into the inner life while an interest is often superficial.

Our Bible lessons may relate pupils more or less personally to the Word of God, the degrees of which may be expressed as follows:

being exposed to the truth
being interested in the truth
doing something about the truth
being controlled by the truth.

If our pupils see no connection between their own needs and the Word, it may be spoken into the air in their vicinity, but will yield little fruit because it doesn't get inside. If it is associated with an interest, they will listen with attention which may lead to something deeper. If they see how the Bible meets a need, they will make some effort to find God's answer. And if they find by experience that the Living God meets other needs, they will continue to appropriate Him inwardly.

But though we have probed to the heart of the problem when we begin with pupils' needs, the process of change is far from automatic. We naturally resist change because it means a new organization of the personality structure that we have been building. It's much easier to continue the line of least resistance than to disrupt old patterns of thinking and acting. If an individual is asked to make too many adjustments at once, he is overwhelmed. We teachers ought to appreciate what is required of a young person who goes back into a godless home and school to live Christ. He needs a great deal of reenforcement from the Lord and the Lord's representatives on earth.

When a man feels the pull of the spiritual world, he will submit to any amount of external routine rather than take himself apart within. It is much easier to fall into the habit of quoting words and assuming that they are meeting God's requirements. If we teachers demand nothing more than words, the pupils will try to quiet their consciences with them. They may be very quick to defend the truth against all comers. But the Lord comes looking for the fruit of the Spirit in life situations. The strength of the heathen religions is that they are intimately bound up with daily life.

Our task as teachers is not so much to motivate as to use the pupils' current motives and values and purposes. They come to us with many needs. As far as possible we should already have discovered these needs, and planned our lesson on the basis of them. If we converse informally with them during presession, we can learn what is uppermost in their thoughts at the moment, and often begin there. On a chalkboard we can write personal questions that point to the Bible content. We can pick up the comments that indicate inner problems. Often personal needs will come out casually in the midst of a lesson and provide rich leading-on values for the next lesson.

Experienced teachers who observe young teachers are often dismayed at the number of excellent leads given by the pupils that go unheeded by the teacher. Questions and comments and suggestions that would lead to thrilling discussions and projects are not even heard. The teacher is so absorbed by the content, he's so uncertain of the sequence of points in his outline, that he isn't teaching content to people, he's just teaching content. He expects the pupils to hear what he says, but he doesn't hear what they say. Is that fair? If pupils' inner needs and ideas and suggestions are woven into the lesson, it will penetrate to the mainsprings of action.

Either we'll seek to meet our pupils' needs by means of the lesson, or they themselves will meet them in a way that will disrupt or negate the lesson. What the pupils want to learn is as important as what the teachers want to teach.

LEARNING AS AN ACTIVE PROCESS

Overheard in a first-grade class:

Teacher: Dickie, what am I going to do with you? The closing bell has rung, and your picture isn't colored, and you don't know your memory verse. I don't suppose you have learned a thing today. Now why is that, Dickie?

Dickie: Well, you made me sit down and be still, and you told me to be quiet and listen, and you *teached* me and *teached* me and *teached* me until I couldn't *learn* anything![14]

'Lizbeth was just seven and she loved school. Her dolls sat in chairs and read and counted and did all the happy things that 'Lizbeth did in school.

Aunt Edith, who lives at 'Lizbeth's house, was a teacher, who often got tired of the reading and counting and other lessons that had to be taught, so one day she offered a suggestion for a new play for the dollies. "Why not play Sunday school, 'Lizbeth? I should think your dollies would like the change."

"No," said the little lady, "my dollies are going to be educated. All we do in our Sunday school is sit and listen, and they'd never learn anything just doing that."

That gave Aunt Edith, who taught Sunday school as well as day school, a lot to think about.[15]

LETTING PUPILS IN ON THE ACTIVITY

Through sermon after sermon, Bible lecture after Bible lecture, are the churches training "professional listeners" who become expert at tuning out what isn't vital to them personally? It is estimated that only about one-fourth of a congregation is really listening to the preacher at any one time. When people are also "talked at" in the so-called teaching sessions, it is no wonder that spiritual results are not more in evidence. Pupils are actually being trained not to listen.

The peculiar genius of teaching is the small intimate group in which overt interaction is possible. Our pupils are often divided into small classes. Why? If we teachers only talked to them, we might as well talk to large groups. The preacher in his sermon should stimulate thinking, but people in the congregation cannot answer him back. Teaching should provide interchange. In teaching, the whole personality should be involved. True is the old saying that we get out of an experience just about what we put into it. There is no such thing as receiving an education. Said Elbert Hubbard, "Education is a conquest, not a bequest; it cannot be given, it must be achieved."

"I will conquer that boy no matter what it may cost him," boasts the misguided teacher; "I will help that boy conquer himself no matter what it may cost me," says the wise teacher. Through the years teachers have been frustrated trying to get pupils to sit still, with pupils frustrated because it is against their nature to sit still. "When teachers do most of the learning, pupils get only the 'dehydrated' product, which is tasteless and dull" (Ruth Bailey). With or without a teacher and a classroom a boy in action is learning.

In transferring the learning process from teacher to pupil, the pupil ought to get half the activity so that he can cash in on the profits. This doesn't imply that the pupil does anything he wants to do or that he goes undisciplined, but he shares with the teacher the responsibility and the activity and the results. He can help devise plans, make his own discoveries in Scripture, evaluate his own efforts. The teacher should do nothing that the pupils can *more profitably* do. We should seek a maximum of self-propulsion, a minimum of absorption of the teacher's words.

What a challenging adventure to help pupils find out for themselves the thrilling possibilities of life in Christ, to guide eager workers rather than to talk to people who are indifferent or actually bored! If people discover the truth for themselves, they are much more ready to obey it.

Teaching by the printed or spoken word is made really effective when indoctrination becomes inspiration, when precept becomes practice, when illustration becomes experience. We learn best by doing the right things, and we can only hope that our information and exhortation will suffice to keep our boys and girls from the wrong kind of experience.[16]

Experience is the best teacher in the sense that her lessons are always learned. Whether or not they are the right lessons is something else again. Experience is a hard teacher, for she gives the test first, the lesson afterward.

The writer of the Book of Hebrews chides his hearers for being dull of hearing and for failing to progress to spiritual maturity (Hebrews 5:11–14). They have had sufficient opportunities to be ready to teach the Word, yet they are still subsisting on the milk of the first principles of eternal truth when they should be ready for strong meat. By reason of use (experience) the mature have their senses exercised (by new understanding and insight) to discern both good and evil (evaluated on the basis of Scriptural norms). Likewise in our churches we should be guiding our young people into experiences that will give them practice in discernment so that they will be maturing as the competent leaders of tomorrow.

Compare the training an athlete gets with that of a spectator at a game. The latter may note the sequence of plays, may shout and cheer at crucial points, may even learn to appreciate some technical skills. But he is not changed by the process. He couldn't duplicate what he saw if he were to get out on the floor or the field. The player on the other hand must plan each strategic move, be very sensitive to the movements of the other players, exercise judgment, take advantage of openings, practice and practice techniques. He comes out of the game a different person because every power has been brought into play. Too long have teachers been the active participants in the game of learning, with the pupils merely spectators. It's time the pupils got into the game.

Somehow, in the process of the development of traditional education, the roles of the student and the teacher have become the reverse of what they should be in participative education. The student should be the primary participant. In traditional education the teachers do what the students should do and the students act as disinterested observers of the process. The college frequently becomes an institution where the students pay tuition to subsidize the teachers, who do the learning. This topsy-turvy condition is well evidenced by a kind of job analysis of the teacher activities. The teacher robs the student of each of these vital experiences: he sets the goals for the students, formulates the questions and problems, evaluates progress, organizes the experience of the student, "integrates" the curriculum, plans the course and the lectures, thinks about the course problems outside of class hours, and does most of the talking. In short, the teachers are the students, the learners, the *participants* in the educative process. It is commonplace to hear teachers say: "I never learned so much as in my first year of teaching." It is questionable how long our society can support institutions where "students" sit and watch teachers learn.[17]

MAKING DISCOVERIES IN THE BIBLE

On Sunday morning Junior High young people sauntered into their Sunday school room buzzing in groups about their new clothes, the fun they'd had the previous evening, the new boy at school, the girl with the new haircut. The room was filled with the cheerful hum of their comments and exclamations until the quiet music began to call them to the worship service. Reluctantly most of the buzz then gave way to passive lethargy while the superintendent and later the teachers talked to them about events that happened long ago and far away, that had little connection with their lives. The leaders made no connections, the pupils saw none. With the exception of some lively choruses that the group sang for fun—they got nothing spiritual out of them—they merely tolerated the proceedings either because it was their habit to come to Sunday school, or they had been trained to be courteous, or on the whole they enjoyed the social situation. The cleverest of them could occasionally get in a sly remark that provoked clandestine merriment from their friends but which the teacher did not notice because he was wholly absorbed with his content. The sound of the closing bell again released the merry chatter right in the middle of the teacher's sentence.

Every week pupils in Sunday school classes ought to be making discoveries in the Bible that are more thrilling than the discoveries in science that are being made in our day. The secrets of the Christ-life that the Lord God is eager to disclose to seeking hearts are more personal and potent than the secrets of the world of nature. If we teachers start right where the pupils are, with their needs, they'll be ready to seek God's answers. Our responsibility then is to guide them in making the discoveries that they need at the moment or that we know they will soon need.

Until a child is able to read, he is unable to search the Scriptures for himself. In the early years the best way of conveying Scriptural truth is the well-told Bible story, in which the teacher himself relives the event so realistically that the boys and girls go through the experience vicariously. No, the children in this case don't actively use their own Bibles, but they can be active in the use of the Bible.

Though the teacher tells the story, the children may listen actively in order to find out something. They should think of it as more than an interesting tale such as they sometimes hear on Saturday at a library story hour. If they have discussed a personal problem that is real to them as the approach to the lesson, they will be discovering how the Bible story meets that need. They will be listening to the story in terms of the need. After the story the teacher won't have to moralize while they fidget; they will be able to draw their own conclusions and make their own applications. After the story of David and Goliath, the teacher may say, "We don't need a sling and pebbles for our giants (that we discussed as the approach to the lesson). How can we today 'be strong in the Lord and in the power of His might'?"

Because children must listen quietly to the Bible story, the rest of the Bible school hour should contain much activity for them. If there is not enough, we can't expect them to sit still to listen to the story. In presession they may examine objects related to the Bible lesson, in worship they actively sing and pray and use familiar Scripture, in expressional work after the story they do something that helps to bridge the gap between knowing and doing God's will.

By the time children become Juniors, they can read well enough to do a lot of experimenting with their own Bibles. Since Bible vocabulary is not the same as that which they read in school, they cannot be depended upon to read well or to get the meaning. They should never be allowed to read before a group if they stumble through a portion haltingly. They should practice whatever they are going to read so that the group hears the Bible read expressively whenever it is read aloud. But if the teacher gives them the setting and problem of a Biblical narrative, they will like to read for themselves the exciting climax to discover the wonderful way in which the Lord worked.

Juniors need plenty of drill in locating the books of the Bible, but they shouldn't get in the habit of using God's written Word mechanically. They derive little benefit from scrambling to see who can first find hit-and-miss verses, rattling off the words with no thought of their meaning. In Bible drills the same mature children usually find the verses first, while the others don't bother to try. Juniors should often look up verses in various parts of Scripture that are related to the problem at hand, and should discuss how these ideas would work out in their own lives during the week.

Junior Highs through adults should regularly experience the thrill of making their own discoveries in Scripture. The teacher's part is to steer them from their personal needs to the passages that meet those needs. When a group begins this type of direct, inductive, laboratory Bible study, the teacher will probably supply sufficient leading questions to bring out all the major answers. As the group gains experience in comparing Scripture with Scripture, it will soon be able to furnish many of the questions also.

The first step in active Bible study is to ask the Author

of the Book for His illumination of the page, for His divine enabling in order that we may know, love, and obey the truth. The passage which answers the need is then placed in its historical setting and read as a whole to get the main thrust. As the student rereads and rereads the whole, he makes concrete factual observations, first about the outstanding characteristics of the passage, then the details. He tries to put himself in tune with the Author of the material, to see as He sees, to feel as He feels. He notes words and phrases that are repeated for emphasis, that are compared, that are contrasted. He asks the questions: What? Why? When? Where? How? He sees interesting relationships take form, and finds out why each section, verse, phrase, and word is where it is, is expressed in a certain way. As he continues to observe, the structure of the literature takes shape. As he makes these factual observations, his perception becomes keener, his discernment sharper.

Not until we have seen what a passage actually says are we ready to interpret its meaning. Marshaling the facts first enables us to get God's message rather than to "prove" our own prejudices.

After students have learned this type of study under the supervision of a teacher, they will be able to prepare their lessons in this way at home during the week. The assignment should be given out in relation to a need that the group currently feels. If students have studied the Bible passage at home, they come to class with the discoveries that they have made, ready to share them with the others. In class the teacher uses their contributions to solve the assigned problem and perhaps others related to it. If no questions remain regarding the initial problem, others involving the same Scripture may be discussed. In class pupils want a new spiritual experience, not the repetition of an old one. This is not difficult since we all have so many needs, with new ones constantly arising.

In answer to questions given out by the teacher or raised

by the pupils, the group continues to search the passage to find facts and relationships that they have missed, to ascertain whether or not observations that they contribute are factually valid, to answer objections to viewpoints that are expressed, to see what light other passages shed on this one, to discuss the practical implications of the truths discovered. One of the first things a group learns is that in an hour or two no one of us begins to get from a Bible passage all its rich meaning. Thus the class members are alert and active intellectually, emotionally, and volitionally as they participate in lively group interaction.

MAKING PUPILS WORK—AND LIKE IT!

"Hi, Miss Reid! You're just the person I'm looking for. Are you free?" The speaker was tall Don Rose, insurance salesman and teacher of the Junior class of boys in Forward Baptist Church.

"Come in, Don," answered Miss Reid.

Don closed the door behind him and pointed his thumb over his shoulder in the direction of the bulletin board in the foyer of the church. "I've just read your new poster," he said, "and decided it was time to talk with you." He was referring to the attractive placard which boldly proclaimed some of the most glaring flaws that were to be found in the Sunday school. In a few words Miss Reid had skillfully painted the characteristics of both a good and a poor teaching situation. Don's inquiry was just what she had been hoping and praying for.

"I've read and reread those words, Miss Reid," he said. "In some spots it describes my class perfectly. I'd like to reach my fellows in the way that that poster says they can be reached."

"What do you like, what don't you like about your lesson period?" encouraged Miss Reid.

"Well, I feel that there was a oneness in the class that you described—the boys and the teacher seemed to be working together—almost unconsciously pulling for the same thing. I'd like an atmosphere like that in my class. The Word of God is so wonderful. The truths there mean so much to me; I want my boys to feel the same way about it. But I feel that I'm just preaching at them. They listen politely for a while, but then I lose them and discipline gets to be a problem. They are so active. It has left me feeling discouraged time and again."

"Look," said Miss Reid, "here's the essence of what you have said. Your aim is to teach the Word; the fellows won't take it when you 'preach' at them. They're full of life and vigor. They want to be active—to be doing things all the time. Can you see any significant relationship in these facts?"

"The Word and their energy," Don thought aloud. "I suppose my problem would be solved if I could harness that energy and get them to expand it in studying the Word."

"Exactly," returned Miss Reid. "That's not easy and yet it can be done."

"I wish you'd show me how," said Don.

"What's your next lesson, Don?"

"We've been working in Mark." Don began thumbing through his Bible. "The next incident coming up is the story of the rich young ruler in chapter 10."

"That's a good one to discuss," said Miss Reid as she reached for her Bible. "The ruler came looking for eternal life. That's what your boys need. Why don't you read through the passage as if you were a Junior. Forget that you're teacher and put yourself in the place of one of the boys."

Don began to read. Almost immediately he looked up. "I don't want to read this," he said. "It doesn't make sense." Don grinned. "That's the way my boys would react. Some of them would stare a little longer at the book, but there would be no interest."

"You're honest enough to see that very real difficulty," encouraged Miss Reid. "How can you make them *want* to read that Bible story, to help them answer some problem of their own, something that's bothering them today?"

Don leaned forward. "Let's see. My boys have it good too, and they aren't bad boys. I could start by describing the rich young man with his houses and lands and servants to wait on him. What could prompt him to kneel in the dust of the road before Jesus, in his fancy clothes? What more could this man want who seemed to have everything? I think the boys could read what he wanted in verse 17. But what would eternal life mean to them?"

"Could one of the sharper boys who is a Christian tell what it means to him?"

"I think Roger could."

"Then you could add the rest, in Junior terms. Maybe, eternal life is the fullest kind of life, the kind that makes you feel good deep down inside, like the life of the mighty Creator who made this tremendous universe with all its galaxies, and its individual people."

"Should the boys read Jesus' answer? Maybe I better express that."

"Yes, for the commandments, you could say don't steal, don't lie, don't cheat, obey your parents."

"Then the class could give the man's answer in verse 20, and find how Jesus felt about the man in 21."

"You're getting the hang of it. It's a real skill to word questions that are not too hard or too easy for a group. Now your boys are ready for the key question that will carry the rest of the lesson, that will direct all we do. How can we express the focal question in the boys' words?"

Don was thinking fast. "Who wouldn't want this full life? The problem is how to get it. So for the boys—if we don't steal or lie or cheat or disobey our parents, is God satisfied with us? How can we have this best kind of life? Hooray! I think that will challenge them!"

"Great! Now they have something to look for, to find out."

"I'll write these important questions so I won't lose them. But the next thing Jesus said made this man hang his head—this rich man who is also called a ruler. What did Jesus say in verse 21? Jesus may not say to us today all that He said to the rich man, but two of those words He is saying to us today. Will we go away sad because we want what we want, or will we pick up Jesus' challenge?"

"Don't feel that the boys need to read everything themselves. You might read 23 and ask how the disciples felt about that in 24. And again you read Jesus' answer in 24-25 and the boys find the disciples' response in 26."

"I could ask why that would be so hard for a rich man. And would anything be too hard for the boys to give up if they love Jesus."

"Then Peter was delighted to discover that the disciples had done something that the rich man couldn't do."

"And Jesus told how He rewards people who follow Him. As the class members read 29-30, they can look for a few words they don't expect. A hundredfold reward *with persecutions!* Who opposes and fights the followers of Jesus? Juniors appreciate the need to be strong to overcome the Enemy."

A big smile came over Don's face as he read verse 31. "Verse 31 is a riddle; Juniors like riddles. How can the first be last, and the last first? How was the rich man first? Last? How are we today?"

Miss Reid was so pleased with the insights that had been discussed. "There's your Bible content outlined," she said.

"At the end I won't have to preach at the boys, the way I usually do. Now I'll ask personal questions about us. Think what happened to you last week. Did you follow Jesus in any way? Did you do some things your own way instead of His best way? Let's make a list of things that boys and girls love more than Jesus. We should get down to nitty-gritty specifics in order to be practical."

"We can't expect them to reform their living overnight, but we can ask them to think of one thing they could do this week to put Jesus first."

"We may not feel like doing these things; they may not be easy. But the Lord will be glad to help us if we ask Him. Let's think what the hard thing might be, and ask Him right now."

"When in the Sunday school hour have you been having your worship service?"

"At the beginning."

"Why not switch it to the end, when the boys are psychologically ready to meet the Lord on the basis of their Bible study? They could sing *Hear the Savior Call, Follow Me* and *I Will Follow Jesus* IF they mean to follow Him. They could study a picture of the rich young ruler, read Mark 10:29–31 in two or three Bible versions, and have a modern illustration of that truth."

"Thanks so much, Miss Reid," Don concluded. "It's going to be fun to give my fellows a workout! Make them work and like it."

GUIDING GROUP DISCUSSION

Recent experience in the field of group dynamics has demonstrated how much can be learned and how much interest generated when young people and adults discuss common problems with open, face-to-face interaction. Basic personality needs are met when we have the opportunity to add our own outlook to a discussion, to voice our questions and doubts without fear of rejection, to hear more than one side of a controversial issue, to find out what problems we share and what others are thinking.

But group discussion requires wise leadership if it is not to waste precious time and degenerate into the pooling of ignorance. The leader establishes a warm spiritual atmosphere by coming well-informed on Biblical and current issues, by insisting that the group be small enough so that the members feel free with each other, by clearly focusing the problem in the direction of Scriptural answers, and by helping each member regardless of his background to make his own contribution. He makes it clear that no person has a monopoly on the Holy Spirit, that spiritual illumination comes primarily from obedience to the Word rather than from intellectual acumen. Every believer has an important place in God's program.

The leader respects every personality, every contribution, every honest question, and helps the group to do so. Every contribution cannot be accepted, but it can be respected. If a group member is assured that the group and the leader accept his whole being as a person, he does not feel crushed or dismayed if one comment or opinion is rejected, for that represents only a small part of him. But if a comment is rejected when he isn't sure of his acceptance as a person, he may not broach an idea again, and the group won't be able to help him because it won't know what he is thinking. If a person is allowed to voice an opinion, even if it is rejected, he usually feels satisfied with the discussion. If not, he has at least looked at the Scriptural basis of the question.

In Christian work a large measure of unity may be expected since all are dependent upon one Holy Spirit, all are studying the relevant Scriptures, and all are learning to appreciate each other. Basic doctrinal issues in Scripture are so clear that all seekers of the truth agree on them. Even on minor questions there is much less difference of interpretation when students approach the Bible factually and objectively. Yet some conflict is to be expected because God's ways are so much higher than man's ways, and traditional ways of thinking and acting have to be disrupted to make room for new ways that are discovered. Group members can make it easy and not hard for others to change by understanding why they have felt as they did and by helping them to ease into the new patterns. Experiments have shown that it is usually easier to change individuals formed into a group than to change any one of them separately.

LEARNING AS A CONTINUOUS PROCESS

As we noted earlier in this chapter, spiritual growth resembles physical growth in that it is usually steady, on-going, continuous. In the home the young child lives in the midst of daily activities of people who are much older than he is. Without the direct intention of anyone to teach him, he is continually learning. What is he learning? The next steps for his own stage of development. Though he is ever imitating, he is not able or interested in imitating everything he sees. Some of the activities of his home hold no meaning for him because they have no connection with his own current stage of growth. He doesn't skip any of the major stages, but takes one after another in a distinct pattern of growth. "First the blade, then the ear, after that the full corn in the ear" (Mark 4:28). Never the ripe fruit before the earlier stages, nor the ear before the blade. These stages of development are part of the orderliness of God's universe that He has ordained in infinite wisdom.

Unlike the plant, the human creature, made in the image of God with self-consciousness and self-determination, may spurt ahead spiritually when he makes significant decisions in the direction of maturity in Christ. He may take several steps at the same time, which is often God's best way, yet even these follow the divine order. At each age level a child should be a healthy mature specimen for that stage. At five he should not regress to the self-centeredness of three, neither should he be expected to act like a ten year old.

At each stage of growth the child is ripe for certain kinds of truth, principles that he can comprehend and act upon. At that time he sees the need for them, they make sense to him, he can weave them into his life. To try to teach them earlier is to waste our time and discourage our pupils. Timing is important.

For example let's take the question of the proper age to teach the books of the Bible. An alert three year old who was the darling of her family was taught to spiel off the names of all the Bible books. She could hardly get her tongue around those awkward sounds that were simply gobbledygook to the small child. But she continued to repeat them for the praise she received. She could show off better with those long names than with anything else she had discovered, so she didn't mind saying them. But when are children ready to learn the books of the Bible with meaning and usefulness? When they are Juniors, when they can read, when they have Bibles of their own, when they've had enough Bible stories so that some of the names are familiar, when they're mature enough to understand the organization of the various sections, when they are gaining some acquaintance with history and geography. It is wise for Primaries to learn to find their way around in the first five books of the New Testament. There is plenty of material here for them to explore, they know many of these stories, can understand what the names of the books mean, and can mark and memorize many of the verses.

But the question may be asked, Don't we need to prepare our pupils for the future? Surely we do, but how? What happens when we try to store their minds with information that they will need at a later date? Unless content can be integrated into one's present thinking and living, it is merely words. What would happen if we removed from a boy's pocket his magnet, flashlight, screwdriver, nail, compass, and substituted things that he'll need when he grows up—driver's license, car insurance, voter's identification, social security card?

How can we best prepare the boy to take his place as a dependable citizen of both his earthly and heavenly country? Can we help him meet tomorrow's needs today? How? By helping him solve today's problems. If he is a spiritually healthy boy of ten today, that's his best guarantee for the future. If he forms habits of relying upon the Lord and obeying Him today, he is headed in the right direction. The best way to insure his being a genuine prayer warrior at fifty is to see to it that he takes to the Lord all the juvenile affairs of life today. It is foolhardy to concentrate on vague future needs at the expense of pressing current needs.

Yet there are some aspects of the future that we all can and should appreciate ahead of time. We can be warned away from disastrous experiences. We can be prepared— to some extent at least—to meet the normal shocks of life. When our friends are going through crises, we may be close enough to them to learn from them. When a loved one or acquaintance dies, we're ready to think seriously about heaven. When an accident happens to someone in our circumstances, we can imagine that it might have happened to us, and we'll heed the warning. When we can visualize a personal experience like taking a job or a trip or adjusting to new family arrangements, the experience is close enough to stir us to get ready for it. If we teachers take advantage of vicarious opportunities like this that have roots in present experience, our pupils will be able to project themselves to some extent into the future.

LEARNING AS A DISCIPLINED PROCESS

When we begin with pupils' needs and proceed according to their developmental level, are we pampering our pupils, are we guilty of "soft pedagogy," will we cover as much content as if we concentrated on subject matter? Yes, we'll be able to teach—actually teach rather than cover— more subject matter, we'll be developing inner control rather than enforcing outer conformity, and we'll be engaging all our pupils' powers.

In their attempts to meet needs, teachers have sometimes erred in lowering the standards of the group to fit the abilities of the least gifted, of the slowest. Then the needs of the average and the superior are not met. Is it possible to challenge everyone to give everything he's got to the lesson at hand? It is if we teach individuals rather than classes. We can make our plans for the average—still the average varies so much! Special attention is then given to those above and below the middle. We must keep before each one a high vision of his untold possibilities in Christ, of the next step toward that vision, not so far ahead that he'll grow discouraged in trying to reach it, but just far enough so that he'll strain every nerve to reach attainable goals.

Formerly many pupils spent their energies trying to get out of work or to get around the teacher or to frustrate his efforts. When pupils accept a goal as worthwhile, as their own, they concentrate their energies on reaching it, they make suggestions as to the best methods of attaining it, they scurry around for the materials they need, they enlist others in the enterprise, they keep evaluating their progress. In other words, the goal is theirs, the Bible class is theirs, not just the teacher's.

Contrast the prodigious labor that a boy puts into the tree house he has decided to make, with a routine job that he considers a boring chore, such as mowing a lawn. The latter is easier, yet he creates much more fuss about it.

When pupils come to church because it is their duty or habit to come, because they are prodded by parents or teachers or friends, or because it affords a pleasant social situation, motivation is weak. It takes strong personality drive to discipline oneself, to hold in check strong natural tendencies. Some other dynamic must take precedence over desire for self-will and self-indulgence. The only motive strong enough to control the old self-life is love for the Lord. Unless divine love is drawing a soul and that soul is responding, self-control cannot be expected.

A new teacher must start out firmly because control is

necessary in any group situation and he cannot depend upon a new group to exercise any control of its own. But the aim of Christian teaching is not mechanical regimentation, rather the development of inner control on the part of all believers. A strong teacher may force outward control, a winning teacher may charm a group into doing as he wishes, a clever teacher may beguile a group. The Christian teacher trains his class to assume more and more responsibility in directing their own affairs under God's authority. A sudden transfer of control would be fatal. At each stage of development the group should be given as much responsibility as it can manage. A good test of a teacher's strength is to watch what happens when he steps out of his room for a minute. Do the "mice" immediately stop their work and begin to play because the "cat" is away, or do they continue their work because it is theirs and they are used to directing their own activities?

Is the Christian curriculum light and thin in content? No, students cover more ground faster when they see the need of it. Then they're eager to learn all they can about their Beloved, they get excited about the insights they discover, they themselves connect ideas in doctrinal systems, with the result that every minute is made to count for eternity. Sometimes a group takes longer to explore for itself a passage than would be required for a teacher to lecture on it, but when they dig into it, it becomes their own, whereas the teacher's words often go in one ear and out the other.

"Teach your disciples to observe all things that I have commanded you," directed our Lord (Matthew 28:18-20). Every believer is entitled to know the whole counsel of God. If we obey the great commission, we'll have to do more than learn to speak the words of truth—we'll also have to acquire the art and science of guiding pupils into the truth.

In summary, effective learning may be defined as an inner, active, continuous, disciplined process under the authority of the Word of God and the control of the Holy Spirit in the direction of maturity in Christ.

Christian teaching is guiding experience and declaring truth. God says, "I will instruct thee and teach thee in the way which thou shalt go: I will guide thee with mine eye" (Psalms 32:8).

WHY IT IS HARD TO PRACTICE THE TRUTH

We all agree that it is much easier to gain a new truth than to practice that truth. Sometimes teachers comment that young children could have longer memory verses than the educators suggest, longer than verses like "obey your parents." What are the implications of these comments? That the children are able to repeat more words? That they are just saying words? How easy is it for them to practice these few words?

Not much research has been done in Biblical psychology. Yet the nature of man is of crucial importance in Christianity. One reason is that the Bible is not a textbook in science; it does not use its terms precisely. But it does yield valuable insights in working with people.

The most common Biblical word in referring to our human makeup is the word *heart,* which is usually used to designate the self, the ego, the essential person. Scripture reflects a healthy respect for the *body* that acts, that relates us to our material world. Our *spirit,* the inner breath that survives death, that relates us to God, is dead until the Holy Spirit quickens it in regeneration.

The term *soul* has no clear-cut designation for us today. Many exegetes hold that it refers to the mind, emotions, and will that relate us to our social world. The problem is which of these three aspects of human nature will have control over the others. Which of the three should have the upper hand, and which actually does in individuals?

Our *emotions* clamor to be in control so that life can be

as easy and pleasant as possible. We can neither deny nor rely on feelings. They energize, are the natural mainsprings of action. They add color, heights, and depths to life. Their pressures give power to the whole being. They can even compel the mind to supply rationalizations for what they want to do. They can also be fickle, can distort reality, can carry away the other aspects of life. They must be disciplined. They cannot be intellectualized away.

For most people *mind* is not as directive as they like to think. It is seldom adequate to move to action. Knowledge may puff up. We cannot find God by reasoning, though, most amazingly, He has enabled us to think His thoughts after Him. God usually gains access to man's inner being through his mind by means of written revelation.

God has given man a *will* that should be strong enough to integrate the whole being by making decisions in the light of the whole for the good of the whole being. This human nature finds very hard to do. For spirit, body, mind, and emotions often disagree on what is good. They all have their own outlooks and interests. Will must get it all together, must try to unify the pulling and hauling of the other parts. It must keep a balance between being independent and being programed, must be free within legitimate authority. Will must keep priorities and principles clear, attitudes and habits disciplined. This isn't easy.

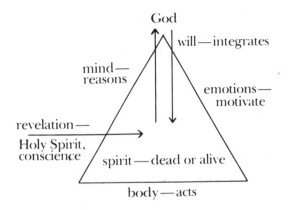

Unregenerate man often lives in conflict because when he is out of tune with his Maker, he is usually out of sorts with himself and his world. How does he get back into right relationships? Probably through his mind as some witness communicates the truth of written revelation. The Holy Spirit without and his conscience within testify that Scripture is true. When he makes the slightest overture to the Living God, the loving Father answers and keeps seeking the lost. If the Spirit reveals the Savior, the mind avers that this is sensible, and the will can decide to commit its being to its Creator. If the emotions are exuberant over becoming a child of the Most High, the feeling is tremendous! But it may be that the emotions are not excited about a life with a cross in it, that is not always strewn with roses. The body too may be opposed; it may be tired or sick or sleepy.

Can the will be strong enough to hold its being together with the emotions pouting or indifferent? Yes, for God Himself works in us to will and do His good pleasure (Philippians 2:13). If we put our weak will on His strong will, He is strong enough to hold it there. If we ask Him to will and do in us, He takes control of the unconscious depths beyond our control. If we are tied only to the Lord, and are one with the Spirit, He will overpower our lower nature. We can be inwardly renewed each day (2 Corinthians 4:16) to experience the good, acceptable, and perfect will of God (Romans 12:2). As we move in His direction, our emotions gradually come to enjoy the process too, until they rejoice in fulness of LIFE. When one's whole being is enthusiastically moving toward the Lord, that is LIFE indeed. Nothing is so attractive or fruitful as wholeheartedness.

Still one of the greatest mysteries of the universe is how the material and the immaterial parts of us can interact with each other when they have no elements in common.

Now we see why it is so difficult to practice the truth that we easily understand. The will must be able to get the mind, emotions, and body to move as the Spirit directs. Unless we teachers involve the whole persons in our classes, they may give assent to our teaching but remain unchanged in conduct. The will of a child must be gradually bent but not broken; he will need all the strength of will he can muster to stand for God in this wicked world.

VII

AUTHORITY AND CREATIVITY

As the Christian teacher seeks to guide experience and declare truth, how are experience and truth related? What is his authority? Is it experience? What kind of experience does he desire? Is truth the authority? What is truth?

CHRISTIAN AUTHORITY

In the thinking of the world of our day, authority, or that which is duly sanctioned, is sometimes said to reside in experience, sometimes in the church, sometimes in social evaluation, sometimes in history. The Christian's authority is the Word of God, the written and Living Word.

In what sense is the Bible the written Word of God? Those who accept the continuity of New Testament and Reformation theology hold the Scriptures to be the special divine revelation of our sovereign Creator-Redeemer. This self-revealing God gave mankind accurate ideas about Himself and His grace in words as the logical symbol of communication, words describing both concepts and experiences. Concepts or doctrines alone would be difficult for man to understand. Experiences alone would be difficult for man to interpret. But doctrines and experiences together teach man as he is able to comprehend—not all, but some of God's infinite character. We would be God if we could understand all of God's counsel.

But what we can understand gives us an accurate, rational, self-consistent world view. In special revelation we have the rational integration of our deep problems of the relation of the changeless to the changing, of the temporal to the eternal.

Because our God is the sovereign Creator-Redeemer, the miraculous is a logical part of His nature. Though He used human instruments for the writing of His Word to man, He superintended that record to keep it from error. Though the writers gave expression to their own temperaments and burdens, yet He "prepared them and illuminated them and energized them." Though He did not use them mechanically as mere pens in His hand, yet He wrote His own Word through them. The result is that we have a miraculous Book, verbally inspired and inerrant in the original writings, and even in its transmission through the centuries kept from error in all essentials.

When the honest seeker after truth is guided by the Holy Spirit of God who bore along the writers of Scripture, when he interprets the language naturally in its setting and context, frail humanity is able to think the very thoughts of God after Him! This revelation of God is valid whether or not men read it, heed it, accept it, or reject it. It records actual historical events though the context indicates that some of it is figurative and symbolic. Again and again in Scripture we are commanded to teach the Word.

This divine Book speaks of miraculous divine events. The infinite God Himself deigns to come down to earth Himself in the Person of the Son in order to redeem from the curse of sin those who receive Him. God the Son Himself stooped to become man through the instrumentality of a virgin birth, He gave Himself a substitutionary atonement for the guilt of the whole world, and then broke the bonds of death in an unheard-of resurrection! This same Jesus will also return physically in power and great glory.

The Almighty also does divine exploits through men, mere men who obey Him. Most amazing experiences are narrated of ordinary men, all dependent upon the objective reality of redemption in Christ.

Through the words of the Bible all mankind is invited to come to the Person who is the focus of history. Without money, without merit, the highest to the lowest of earth are bidden to receive new life, eternal life, the very life of the Savior Himself, in supernatural regeneration. Receiving Christ opens up marvelous possibilities for personal maturity, adventure, and productivity. Only in Christ can the human being fulfill the destiny for which he was created. Only within the framework of the objective authority of the Word of God can subjective experience be fruitful and rewarding.

The major problem in relation to authoritative revelation is to get it accepted by each new generation. This acceptance cannot be forced, it must not be superficial. *Authoritarian* method is often associated with our *authoritative* message. If the Bible is taught in the spirit of "Here it is; you take it because I say so"; if it is taught by stereotyped, rote-memory methods, what happens? Instead of accepting it as their own conviction, young people rebel against this affront to their free will. Likewise we fail if we try to transmit Scripture by transmissive methods, if we only ask young people to parrot it back to us in the same form in which we gave it.

Because Christ and the Bible are the same "yesterday, today, and forever," well-meaning Christian people sometimes feel that nothing in relation to the Bible ever changes. What was good enough for our fathers is good enough for us, is the attitude. If our fathers sat and endured, no matter what pastor or teacher went wandering in what wilderness, why shouldn't we? If the young people of old were trained to copy old patterns instead of creating new ones, why shouldn't our young people?

Acceptance of God's revelation as authoritative can be effected only by clear teaching and exemplary living on the part of the older generation and by satisfying experiences on the part of the younger generation. From his earliest years the child should personally hear GOD'S VOICE, sometimes thunderous, sometimes still and small, but continually he should hear THUS SAITH THE LORD spoken in terms of his own daily life. He should grow up feeling that the center of life is not his small I, his ego, his self that wants its own way to its own destruction. But rather that the center of life is THE BIG I, THE GREAT I AM, who alone knows best, who alone is able to implement His ideas. If that child's parents and teachers live joyfully under God's authority, bow to His decrees even when they cannot understand them, if they demonstrate daily that His is the best life, and require of the child not their own stronger will but rather the sovereign divine will, he will gradually recognize the impotence of his own nature and the right of the Great Governor of the universe to be worshiped and obeyed. From his earliest years too he can experience the deep inner relaxation of being in harmony with his Maker, and the excitement of working creatively with the Source of Life Himself.

CHRISTIAN CREATIVITY

A. W. Tozer expresses the urgent need for sanctified thinkers:

A religious mentality characterized by timidity and lack of moral courage has given us today a flabby Christianity, intellectually impoverished, dull, repetitious and to a great many persons just plain boresome. This is peddled as the very faith of our fathers in direct lineal descent from Christ and the apostles. We spoon-feed this insipid pabulum to our inquiring youth and, to make it palatable, spice it up with carnal amusements filched from the unbelieving world. It is easier to entertain than to instruct, it is easier to follow degenerate public taste than to think for oneself, so too many of our evangelical leaders let their minds atrophy while they keep their fingers nimble operating religious gimmicks to bring in the curious crowds.

Well, I dare to risk a prophecy: The sheep are soon going to become weary both of the wilted clover we are giving them and the artificial color we are spraying over it to make it look fresh. And when they get sick enough to leave our pastures, the Pope, Father Divine, Mrs. Eddy and their kind will find them easy victims.

Christianity must embrace the total personality and command every atom of the redeemed being. We cannot withhold our intellects from the blazing altar and still hope to preserve the true faith of Christ.[18]

"Dewey-eyed" religious educators who reject divine authority contend that it stops the process of earnest search and curtails the spirit of adventure. A group may be exploring various solutions to a problem by uncovering many kinds of data and insights—until they come upon the words, "thus saith the Lord." If they must accept His mandate whenever He speaks on a subject, how can we expect them to develop initiative and resourcefulness in meeting the needs of their day?

What if God's Word does stop the process of earnest search! When the Eternal One furnishes the answers that are inherent in the very structure of the universe, why not stop when we have discovered them? What would be the value of continuing the search? There are plenty of problems that God hasn't answered in His Book. He has left for us so many needs, so many problems that we can't begin to solve them!

Why waste our precious energy and limited time on mysteries that have already been explained? How discouraging to spend one's life formulating systems that will soon be discarded by the next generation! How encouraging to know that we can build structures that will endure! In His revelation God has given us all the insights that we need to know, all we cannot find out for ourselves. What security is like that of working with the Creator Himself!

Therefore let's rest in what God has already given and tackle the pressing needs that lie all about us. When we encounter needs and problems, let's first find all the relevant principles and examples, then use our own minds that He has created, under the guidance of His Spirit. He has by no means given us pat formulas for everything—step 1, step 2, step 3. He has given us room to move and a foothold sure (Psalms 18:36 MOFFATT). He asks of us both obedience and initiative. In the words of Cyrus H. K. Curtis, "There are two kinds of men who never amount to much: those who cannot do as they are told, and those who can do nothing else." Rather than discouraging our own efforts, divine authority ought to multiply them.

Should Christians be more or less colorful and productive than other people? Does the dull, drab personality reflect the Christian life? Where are the Christian scholars who are forging new frontiers of knowledge based on Scriptural foundations? Where are the writers who give vision of the Christian pathway from the realistic existential situation to exalted heights in Christ? Who will conduct the scientific experiments? Where are the educators who are working out on the growing edge of the field? Who will produce the curriculum materials?

Obedience to divine authority demands Christian creativity. This term is sometimes frowned upon by Christians because worldlings use it to oppose that which is authoritative. In a naturalistic framework that denies supernature, in which all is relative with no absolutes, the secularist holds that knowledge as well as method arises from within the group process, that what is true for one group in one situation may not be true for another in another situation. Such relativism is at swords' points with Christianity.

But the word "create" is a Scriptural word which belongs to Christians in its own distinctive sense. In the beginning God created the heavens and the earth (Genesis 1:1); at the end of the age He will create new heavens and a new earth (Isaiah 65:17). By His Spirit He creates all living things, and renews the face of the earth (Psalms 104:30). He creates the new man in Christ Jesus, in righteousness and true holiness, unto good works (Ephesians 2:10, 4:24).

This same Creator says to man, ". . . work out your own salvation with fear and trembling. For it is God which worketh in you both to will and to do of his good pleasure" (Philippians 2:12,13). He said to Joshua, "Arise, go across Jordan to the land I have given you. Every place that your feet shall tread upon I have given you. Only be strong and very courageous" (Joshua 1:2). The psalmist said to the Lord, "For with thee is the fountain of life: in thy light shall we see light" (Psalms 36:9). And ". . . all my springs are in thee"—all my fresh ideas are in Thee (Psalms 87:7). It is He who has wrought all our works in us (Isaiah 26:12). In the Book of Isaiah the Lord God asks, "Wherefore, when I came, was there no man?" (Isaiah 50:2) "And he saw that there was no man, and wondered that there was no intercessor . . ." (Isaiah 59:16).

Today as in every age the Lord is seeking individuals through whom He can carry out His purposes. Through whom can He pray and plan and execute today? Through believers who are not only dead to sin, but fully alive in Christ. Christian creativity is God still at work today by His

Spirit through His people, working out His purposes on the basis of the Given, with each situation distinctive. It is still God today who does the creating. Anything we do in the flesh might better be left undone. So our part is to receive Him and to cooperate in whatever He is waiting to do through us.

God has set every believer in the body of Christ as it has pleased Him, each one with his own talents and contribution to make to the whole. Though there are diversities of gifts, ". . . the manifestation of the Spirit is given to every man to profit withal" (1 Corinthians 12:4,7). Each is necessary. Each has a place that no one else can fill so well. Christ wants to reflect His own attributes through the particular combination of traits that each of us possesses. If we would have needed anything more for a true demonstration of Himself, He would have given it to us. No matter how great or how small our talents, we are to develop and use them. Then there would be no lack in the body, but it would be growing progressively stronger and more mature.

What a shame that many people never know what Christ could do in them, never realize their dormant potentialities! In the words of Oliver Wendell Holmes, "Alas for those that never sing, but die with all their music in them!" They have never been released from their old natures, never know the glorious freedom of the sons of God! Christ said, "If ye continue in my word, then are ye my disciples indeed; And ye shall know the truth, and the truth shall make you free" (John 8:31,32).

We Christians need not imitate the worldlings around us; we can be lifted above the things of earth by letting the Spirit kindle our minds and imaginations, that we may know by experience what is God's very best for us (Romans 12:2). The will of the Lord for us should grow increasingly clearer, being illuminated more brightly each day of our lives (Proverbs 4:18). Whoever is refreshed by the Spirit will never feel unsatisfied, but the fulness of the Spirit will become in us a fountain of overflowing freshness, bubbling up into the life of God (John 4:14). Then we'll say with the psalmist, "I can't keep to myself the joy that I feel; I must express my gladness concerning my Lord; my speech flows along very readily" (Psalms 45:1). Then we'll produce the books and materials that our world so sorely needs.

Says Oswald Chambers:

> When once God's Redemption comes to the point of obedience in a human soul, it always creates. If I obey Jesus Christ, the Redemption of God will rush through me to other lives, because behind the deed of obedience is the Reality of Almighty God.[19]
> The inner reality of Redemption is that it creates all the time. As the Redemption creates the life of God in us, so it creates the things belonging to that life. Nothing can satisfy the need but that which created the need. This is the meaning of Redemption—it creates and it satisfies.[20]

THE EXAMPLE OF DAVID IN SCRIPTURE

Probably the most creative personality that Scripture presents is the man David. How much poorer we would be without his psalms! In the one Book that is God-breathed, how many details of the story of his life are included! Why would David's life and contribution be particularly helpful to succeeding generations? What caused his life to be so productive? Did God's authority bind him or free him? What can we learn about Christian creativity from him?

We first note what a rich, varied life David lived. He was shepherd, leader of refugees, warrior, king, and poet. He had a healthy background of heredity and training, and was not afraid of new experiences. We infer from the many references to nature in the psalms that as he cared for his sheep in God's wide world of nature, he early experienced personal dealings with the Creator of all living, growing things. As a lad we see him sitting under a shady tree playing his harp while the sheep graze nearby. With time for private meditation as well as action, we hear him singing his own majestic songs to the Lord:

When I consider thy heavens, the work of thy fingers, the moon and the stars, which thou hast ordained;

What is man, that thou art mindful of him? and the son of man, that thou visitest him?

For thou hast made him a little lower than the angels, and hast crowned him with glory and honour.

Thou madest him to have dominion over the works of thy hands; thou has put all things under his feet:

All sheep and oxen, yea, and the beasts of the field;

The fowl of the air, and the fish of the sea, and whatsoever passeth through the paths of the seas.

O LORD our Lord, how excellent is thy name in all the earth! (Psalms 8:3–9).

The next minute he is jumping up to rescue a lamb from the jaw of a lion.

We next note David's warm, outgoing personality that attracted people. His name means "beloved." Surely he was a great lover, both of God and of man. In both Old and New Testaments he is called a man after God's own heart (1 Samuel 13:14, Acts 13:22); the Book of Acts adds that he will do all God's will. The dominant tone of his life was wholehearted devotion to the Lord. Though he committed grave sins, he judged no one more harshly than himself and mourned over his guilt before the Lord. In the record there is no trace of a rebellious spirit.

The spontaneity of his devotion is illustrated by an incident that took place during his exile (2 Samuel 23:15–17). In the cave of Adullam he wished aloud for a drink of the water of the well of Bethlehem, the cool refreshing water that he remembered enjoying as a boy. When his three mighty men broke through the garrison of the Philistines and brought him this water, he could not think of drinking it. Water that had endangered their lives was too precious for him to drink. Sacrificially he poured it out unto the Lord.

This incident also shows the love that his followers had for him because he merited their affection and loyalty. When he escaped to Adullam, four hundred men went with him, later two hundred more joined him (1 Samuel 22:1,2; 23:13). When Saul first saw David, he loved him greatly (1 Samuel 16:21). Jonathan delighted much in David (1 Samuel 19:2). After Saul and Jonathan were killed in battle, David was the people's natural choice for king as well as God's choice (2 Samuel 5:1,2).

The Word of God goes into detail to describe David's outstanding act of kindness to Saul's lame son (2 Samuel 9), his kindness to Shimei of Saul's family who insulted David as he was fleeing from Jerusalem (2 Samuel 19), and his grief over the loss of his son Absalom (2 Samuel 18). But his warm emotion coupled with indulgence at a time of leisure and prosperity got him into trouble with Bathsheba (2 Samuel 11). This man who in righteous indignation had ordered others to be killed for not respecting human life (2 Samuel 4), himself plotted the death of Bathsheba's husband, one of his own mighty men who was performing his duty in the army. Moreover Deuteronomy 17:17 warned that kings were not to multiply wives for themselves. As the inevitable consequence of this domestic crime, his sensitive soul suffered bitter anguish as his first son by Bathsheba died and his own children and trusted friends committed against him the same sort of treachery as he had committed against Bathsheba's husband.

Though warm-hearted David often acted spontaneously in love and kindness, the record asserts that in many decisions he looked to God's authority rather than acting on his own initiative. Although he was anointed by Samuel to be king over God's people, he would not take it into his own hands to get rid of the king, but lived for years in exile in the wilderness. He respected the Lord's anointed and the Lord's timing. In his conflict with Goliath he relied not upon the king's strong armor, but upon his knowledge of God's will and the experience of God's deliverance in the past. ". . . who is this uncircumcised Philistine, that he should defy the armies of the living God?" he shouted (1 Samuel 17:26). "The Lord that delivered me out of the paw of the lion, and out of the paw of the bear, he will deliver me out of the hand of this Philistine" (1 Samuel 17:37).

When David received word that the Philistines were fighting and robbing the town of Keilah, he inquired of the Lord, "Shall I go and smite these Philistines?" (1 Samuel 23:1–5). The Lord answered, "Go . . . and save Keilah." When his men protested in fear, David again inquired of the Lord, who answered, ". . . I will deliver the Philistines into thine hand." When this same enemy pitched against Saul and Saul inquired of the Lord, ". . . the Lord answered him not, neither by dreams, nor by Urim, nor by prophets" (1 Samuel 28:6).

But David's patience with Saul was exhausted before the Lord's. It was not easy in the wilderness when he was being continually pursued to provide for his two wives and the large band of outlaws that followed him. In a fit of panic and mistrust he said to himself, "I shall now perish one day by the hand of Saul. I may as well escape to the Philistines; then Saul will stop hunting me" (1 Samuel 27:1). This he did without consulting the Lord, in spite of the promises of the Lord. Achish, king of Gath, now received him because of his sizable following, and trusted him. He gave David the country town of Ziklag where the Israelites would have more freedom than in the royal city. But in the land of the enemy David continually had to practice deceit. When he raided the border tribes of the south country that were in alliance with the Philistines, he was compelled to slay every man and woman lest someone bring back a report to

Achish. When the king asked him where he had been raiding, he pleased the king by answering that he had plundered his own people. It was of the mercy of the Lord that the lords of the Philistines refused to permit David to go out to battle with them against Israel (1 Samuel 29).

When David and his men returned from this battle, they found that the Amalekites had smitten Ziklag, burned it, and taken captive its women and children (1 Samuel 30). So distressed were they that they wept until they could weep no more. The men were so grieved to be bereft of their families that they even spoke of stoning David. In this crisis David reverted to his true center; he encouraged himself in the Lord his God. He inquired of the Lord whether or not he should pursue the troop. The Lord answered that he should pursue and that he would surely recover all his possessions.

After his home in Ziklag had been burned and he had mourned the death of Saul and Jonathan, he asked the Lord, "Shall I go up into any of the cities of Judah?" (2 Samuel 2:1). The Lord said, "Go up." But David didn't know just where to go. When he asked about the particular city, the Lord specified exactly, "Unto Hebron." Because he was in the Lord's place at the Lord's time, the men of Judah there anointed him king over Judah. After David's general murdered Saul's general, David wept at his grave (2 Samuel 3:32). When David refused to eat till the sun went down, this pleased the people, ". . . as whatsoever the king did pleased all the people" (2 Samuel 3:36). After the murder of Ish-bosheth all the tribes of Israel came to David at Hebron and anointed him king over Israel (2 Samuel 5:3).

After his anointing over all the tribes we read that David and all his men went to Jerusalem, the strategically situated natural capital of the land (2 Samuel 5:6,7). This time the record makes no mention of any inquiry of the Lord. Apparently God's people deemed it a reproach to leave to foreigners this stronghold in the midst of the land. Joshua had defeated its king (Joshua 10), Judah had set it on fire but failed to capture its king (Judges 1:8). The Jebusites considered the hill impregnable, but David took it. And he became greater and greater, for the God of hosts was with him (2 Samuel 5:10). He realized that the Lord had made him king over Israel and had exalted his kingdom for the sake of His people (2 Samuel 5:12).

When the Philistines heard that David had been made king of the united kingdom, they all came up to seek him (2 Samuel 5:17–25). In great numbers they poured into the valley of Rephaim, cutting him off from the northern tribes. Though he was now king, David did not feel confident of God's victory over his old enemy with whom he had taken refuge. He asked the Lord, "Shall I go up against the Philistines?" The Lord answered, "Go up, for I will surely deliver the foe into your hand."

Once again the Philistines came up and spread themselves in the valley of Rephaim. Again David inquired of the Lord. This time the Lord replied, "Don't go up after them, but go around and come upon them opposite the balsam trees. When you hear the sound of marching in the tops of the balsam trees, go out to battle, for I have gone out before you to smite the host of the Philistines." After that God's people enjoyed peace for ten years.

As David began to set his kingdom in order, he sought to make Jerusalem the spiritual capital as well as the political capital of his realm. He said democratically to the commanders of thousands and of hundreds, "If it seems good to you, and if it is the will of the Lord our God, let's gather together all our people and bring again the ark of the Lord to our city, for we neglected it in the days of Saul" (1 Chronicles 13). Since this idea seemed right in the eyes of all the people, all Israel went to the house of Abinadab in Kirjathjearim to get the ark of God. They set it upon a new cart, driven by the sons of Abinadab, Uzza, and Ahio.

As they journeyed, David and all Israel rejoiced before God with songs and musical instruments. When they reached the threshingfloor of Chidon, Uzza put out his hand to hold the ark because the oxen stumbled. The anger of the Lord was kindled against Uzza because he touched the holy ark, and he paid for his error with his life.

The language used to describe David's response to this judgment of the Lord leads us to infer that David was ignorant of the Lord's reason for judgment. We read that David was angry and afraid of the Lord that day. "How can I bring the ark of God home to me?" he asked. Instead of continuing the journey, he took the ark aside to the house of Obed-edom the Gittite. While it remained there for three months, the Lord blessed Obed-edom and all that he had. This blessing signified that the Lord accepted David's idea; it was a good idea, but he was responsible for knowing and obeying the law in relation to his idea. It is necessary not only to do the Lord's will, but to do it in the Lord's way.

As the king reflected upon God's harsh judgment, he no doubt remembered or discovered that part of the law which prescribed precisely how the ark of God was to be carried and what would happen if even the priests touched it (Numbers 4:2,15; 7:9). So he again assembled all Israel, including the priests and Levites, and said to the Levites, "No one but you may carry the ark of God (1 Chronicles 15). Because you didn't carry it the first time, as God had ordained, he broke forth upon us." Then the priests sanctified themselves and carried the ark of God upon their shoulders with poles without touching it, as the Lord had commanded Moses.

Soon David had an even better idea (2 Samuel 7). He said to Nathan the prophet, "It doesn't seem right for me to dwell in a palace of cedar when the ark of God dwells in a tent." Apparently Nathan at once concurred in this good idea. He answered, "Do all that is in your heart, for God is with you."

But that night the word of the Lord came to Nathan, "Go,

tell my servant David that he shall not build me a house"
(1 Chronicles 17). Through Nathan the Lord rejected
David's proposal so delicately that it is difficult to single out
the sentence that contains the direct negative. To David the
Lord said, "Have I ever asked my people why they haven't
built me a house? I took you from the pasture to be prince
over my people, and I will make you a great name. Moreover I will plant my people, that they may dwell securely.
And I will build you a house, and establish the kingdom of
one of your sons. He shall build a house for me, and I will
establish his throne forever."

Later at the dedication of the temple Solomon said, "The
Lord said to David my father, 'Thou didst well that it was
in thine heart to build a house for my name' " (2 Chronicles
6:8). This too was a good idea.

In response to the Lord's reply David went in and sat
before the Lord and said, "Who am I, O Lord God, and
what is my house that thou hast brought me so far? And
thou hast even spoken of thy servant's house for a long time
to come. Thou art great, O Lord God; there is none like
thee. What other nation on earth is like thy people, whom
thou didst redeem for thyself! Do as thou hast said, and let
thy name be magnified forever."

In both 2 Samuel 8 and 1 Chronicles 18 the words that
follow hard upon this prayer denote bold decisive action.
After this David defeated the Philistines and subdued them
for the last time. He defeated the Moabites and put them
under tribute. As he went to recover his border at the river
Euphrates, he smote Hadarezer, king of Zobah. When the
Syrians of Damascus came to help Hadarezer, he killed
twenty-two thousand of them and put them under tribute.
The Lord gave David victory wherever he went. When the
king of Hamath heard that he had defeated all the host of
Hadarezer, he congratulated David because he had often
been at war with Hadarezer, and he brought David vessels
of silver, gold, and brass.

As a preface to these wars the sacred record makes no

mention of inquiry of the Lord. Probably God's promise
that He would plant His people securely and establish their
kingdom forever coupled with David's high worship experience impelled him to enter boldly into the heritage that
God had long ago promised His people. His old enemy the
Philistines were the first to be conquered. Great treasures
of gold, silver, and brass that David captured in his wars
were dedicated for the building of the temple though David
himself was not to do it because he was a warrior who had
shed blood (1 Chronicles 28:3). He also gave Solomon the
pattern of all the porches and courts and rooms of the
temple that he had by the Spirit. All this he made clear in
writing from the hand of the Lord (1 Chronicles 28:11,-
12,19).

Another sin committed by David was a selfish idea
prompted probably by pride and lack of trust (2 Samuel
24). Probably he wanted to know how many people he
ruled over in Israel and Judah. The whole nation suffered
seriously, yet the justice of the Lord is seen in the words of
2 Samuel 24:1, ". . . the anger of the Lord was kindled
against Israel." 1 Chronicles 21:1 (RSV) says, "Satan stood
up against Israel, and incited David to number Israel."
Joab, who is not known for the purity of his motives,
remonstrated with David that he should not bring this guilt
upon Israel, but David's word prevailed against him and
against the captains of the host. After Joab had gone
through all the land, David's heart smote him, for God was
displeased, and He had to smite His people. David then
said to the Lord, "I have sinned greatly, but take away the
iniquity of thy servant."

Through Gad, David's seer, God offered David three
awful alternatives. Rather than fall into the hand of men,
David preferred to fall into the hand of the Lord, for he was
assured that His mercy was great. When the destroying
angel stretched forth his hand to destroy Jerusalem, the
Lord stopped him at the threshingfloor of Ornan. When
David saw the angel who was smiting the people, he said to

the Lord, "It is I who have sinned and done very wicked-
ly. But these sheep, what have they done? Let thy hand, I
pray thee . . . be against me and against my father's
house. . . ." (1 Chronicles 21:17, RSV).

The angel of the Lord commanded Gad to tell David to
rear an altar to the Lord on that spot in order to avert the
plague. The owner of the threshingfloor offered to give
David the floor and animals for sacrifice to the Lord, but
David insisted on buying them, saying, "I will not offer to
the Lord my God that which cost me nothing."

Though David sinned like the rest of us, he judged no
one more rigorously than himself. What comfort we derive
from his psalms of penitence, anguish, and conflict as well
as those of joy and deliverance!

Because he was usually activated by the highest of motives—for the Lord's great name's sake, for His Word's
sake, and for His people's sake—his heart usually over-
flowed with praise and thanksgiving. Because of nobility of
character and ideals that were rooted firmly in the Creator
Himself, his poetic temperament was expressed in beautiful vivid language. His individual initiative was encouraged
by God when he was acting within the will of God. But
ignorance of the will of God was no excuse for going ahead
on his own. And he was not to carry out an approved
project in his own way or to take on one that the Lord had
ordained for his son. The Lord allowed him to prepare the
costly materials for the temple and the Lord gave him its
blueprint. But his work was to extend the kingdom to the
bounds set by God, set up a stable government (2 Samuel
8:15), establish patterns of spiritual worship, and provide
worship materials. God had ordained his particular contribution, as He has for all of us; he need not usurp another
man's.

PRODUCTIVE CHRISTIAN PERSONALITY

Where are the Davids and Solomons through whom the
Lord can accomplish His purposes for our day? When He

anoints a young person for service today, He chooses, as of old, someone who is on intimate terms with Himself, whose own life He has filled to overflowing, for it is the "overflow of heart that gives the lips full speech." Every advance that we seek to make in service means that the white light of God's holiness must be turned more fully into the inner recesses of our own personal lives. It has been said that God's greatest problem is His people. It's futile to try to develop the *gifts* of the Spirit (1 Corinthians 12) before we have developed the *graces* of the Spirit (Galatians 5:22,23). What we are is more important than what we do. Have we truly died to self? Are we fully alive in Christ? If the Son of God is manifest in our mortal flesh, the sweet savour of His resurrection life will emanate to those around. If we are in constant contact with Him, the Power from on high will be present to convict and convert and conquer.

No matter what our vocation, no matter whether our temperament be retiring or outgoing, every believer in Christ should be a creative, colorful person. If Life Himself is pulsing through every nerve and the eternal Creator is manifesting Himself in us, how can life be dull and drab? Christian life should radiate creative faith and love.

One of the most tragic things in this world is the number of unlovely good people in it. One does not question for a moment the reality of their goodness. Yet the pity of it is, the more you know them the less you want to be with them, the less even you want to be like them. They have goodness, but they lack love. Dwight L. Moody once said a beautiful thing about Henry Drummond: "Most of us make an occasional excursion into the thirteenth of First Corinthians, but Drummond lived there."[21]

Any of us may improve our personal productivity by observing the following:

1. *Let the Word of Christ dwell in us richly in all wisdom* (Colossians 3:16).

God's truth is to dwell in us in the sense of keeping house in our bodies, of directing activities as master of the household rather than laboring merely as a servant. He is to dwell in us richly, to have full run of the whole house, to control whatever goes on. From God's Word we are to receive our instructions, our daily portions of milk and meat, our needed supplies of grace. Since wisdom is the highest means to the noblest ends, this divine wisdom will enable us to practice as well as to understand the truly fruitful life.

If the Word of God dwells in us as head of the house rather than being confined to one room or to one hour of the day, every aspect of our life will gradually be transformed. Only in God's light can we see light, but that light will glow brighter and brighter as we walk His higher ways. We shall then be continually gaining new insights, observing new relationships, claiming new promises, obeying new commands. Thus life will hold many new experiences that we'll not be afraid to encounter because we're resting secure in the authority of God Himself.

Unless the Word reigns within, God's ways will seem too high for us; we will fear His ideals instead of courageously scaling the heights. God's ways are high, infinitely higher than our ways, yet He doesn't lower His standards one bit in deference to our infirmities. He merely bids us take hold of His strength and wisdom and grace. If we can sight the goal and know definitely how to take each step, one after the other, in the direction of the goal, we need never be discouraged. The mountain peaks of God's program become veiled with clouds to many dear Christian people because they see no path that leads from where they are to such heights. They need leaders who have already climbed the steep ascent and have returned to help them gain their footing at each level.

2. *Let the Spirit of God free us from the flesh, which is constantly clamoring to intrude into spiritual activities, so that we may be tied only to the Lord.*

Only the Christian can be freed from himself to work unhampered with the Creator. Yet how few of us begin to experience this freedom! The chief concern of a Christian is identification with Christ, nothing less. Identification with His death and resurrection, with His active energy working mightily in us. Certain of Him, we may be uncertain of everything else. Are we disconnected from the world fundamentally, or only externally?

Self-will, self-wisdom, and self-activity are our deadliest foes. Though the Lord calls us His friends because He wants us to work intelligently with Him, the energy of the flesh is a traitor. Instead of bowing before His will and wisdom in simple trust and humility, how often we act in pride, which is the deification of self! If we spent more time in the presence of the Lord, we'd have to spend less time on our work.

Though Christ has been originally enthroned in our lives, we often unwarily depose Him. He must often keep back good gifts that He would love to shower upon us, but if He did, we would concentrate on the use of them rather than concentrate on their Giver. He often needs to send trouble, for we human creatures never clasp trouble to our breasts, but always try to escape it, perhaps by fleeing to Himself.

Tragic as it is, the fact remains that Christian work may be the chief usurper of Christ's throne. In this age of hurry and flurry it is much more natural to be busying ourselves about programs than to be waiting upon the Lord. Only the Spirit of Christ can keep Christ in the center of life.

3. *Give the Lord a chance to lead in any direction by not shutting off any possibilities that are consonant with Scripture.*

Very narrow tradition has sometimes been so equated with Scripture that we, God's people, have been kept out of the glorious heritage that should be our present possession. Like the Pharisees of Jesus' day, we have sometimes added to Scripture our own prejudices and interpretations until we read them into the Word instead of discovering what God is actually saying. All truth is God's truth, whether found in Scripture, nature, or experience, and these sources of truth never clash if the false has not been mixed with the true.

Because God's people have been so slow to uncover His secrets, "to have dominion over the earth" as He intends us to, godless men have forged far ahead of us, have studied God's creations, have made valid discoveries, often falsely interpreted on the basis of their own naturalistic assumptions. Without being able to examine closely their scientific process, our people have been inclined to fear and shy away from anything that these naturalists explore. Many years after the disclosure of some discovery, when it is finally evident to all of us that the heathen were merely unearthing God's laws, we gradually adopt for ourselves these truths from unreliable sources.

Is this procedure God's best for His people? Why shouldn't we be out front pioneering in every worthy endeavor? Why should we always be tardily and grudgingly accepting the findings of unbelievers? When graded lessons were first introduced into the Sunday school, evangelicals were heartily opposed to them because in conjunction with them came extra-Biblical lessons. Study of the methods of Christ was opposed because overstress on His humanity came with it. The Scriptures give us foundations and leads for basic principles in education, psychology, sociology that we haven't begun to explore. Each generation ought to be gleaning new insights from the Bible in terms of its own current needs and problems.

An example of our defection is found in the fascinating new field of group dynamics that has received so much attention recently in all the social sciences. After we study the principles of effective group process from secular sources, we go to the Bible to see if this emphasis fits into our framework, and discover that it is indigenous to the very nature of the church. In fact, we Christians ought to function much more harmoniously than other groups because the Holy Spirit moves among us to form the mind of Christ in us. Acts 15 is a classic example of group process. We should have been perfecting group skills since the first century. But we haven't been. And outsiders had to discover them and bring them into the church from outside. Shame on us!

Often young people never achieve their highest and best because the whole range of vocations is not held before them as worthy of a Christian. A few limited so-called "full-time" occupations are the only ones that seem to be approved by their elders. If a young person can best use his divine gifts as a plumber, he should have the privilege of knowing a Christian plumber who is a winsome soul-winner wherever he works. Our outlook should be as narrow but no narrower than the Scriptures themselves.

4. *Keep motivation strong and pure, for that supplies a sense of urgency and responsibility.*

Most of us don't know what we could actually do if we were to be fully activated, with all our powers called forth simultaneously. "The patient dedication of the will counts far more than native ability. Capacity flows more often from desire than desire from capacity." One man with a personal burden will accomplish more than ten with mere interest. The world has had very little opportunity to see what God could do with men who wholly followed Him. If communism can motivate such dedication and sacrifice for the goals of Marxism, should not Christians apprehend that for which they've been apprehended by the Lord of Life Himself?

The only thing that the field of Christian education is full of is needs. Needs stare us in the face everywhere we turn. The few people who are competent in this field can't begin to multiply themselves fast enough. The following are some of the types of Christian creativity needed today— creativity interpreted broadly in its total setting:

Mature Christian lives
Effective daily witness
Use of the Word to best advantage
Everyday good works
Practical decisions
Organization of churches, boards, schools
Teaching people to observe all the truth
Thinking through problems in philosophy and psychology
Writing of literature for many purposes
Illustrating Scriptural truth

A Christian leader must continually check his motives to see why he is doing what he is. At our high moments we begin a project with a vision of the Lord Himself and His commission. The love of Christ constrains us. But in the midst of the wear and tear of personnel problems and organizational confusion, it is very easy to move off center, to wake up finding ourselves unduly concerned about our own reputation and our own rewards. "Never act from motives of rivalry or personal vanity," says Paul to the Philippians, "but in humility think more of each other than you do of yourselves" (Philippians 2:3 PHILLIPS).

5. *Keep problems sharply focused, so that we'll glean from our experiences everything that will help us solve them.*
If we fail to organize and crystallize the problems that come to us from various sources, they remain vague and fragmentary, with the result either that we do nothing about them or we feel uneasy and frustrated. People who are intellectually curious are usually mulling over several

problems at off hours; they have several pots simmering on the back burners of their minds. When a problem confronts them, they try as soon as possible to delve down to the real root of the conflict, to see what factors are involved. Because they keep that problem pointed up in their minds, many unrelated experiences in daily living contribute to insight into its solution. A message on another subject, a conversation at a lunch table, a sentence in a book may furnish valuable source material for that problem.

When an idea comes, write it down. Most people are unable to keep several problems perking at once unless they have an organized place to jot down what comes during the day. Ideas are priceless; don't lose them. In most of our heads they don't seek to return to consciousness, as Herbart thought in terms of association psychology, they tend to escape us. Therefore don't let ideas inch away from you. The more fruitful experiences you have, the broader and richer will be your ideas. The more you integrate and use the ideas you get, the more creatively you'll be able to combine them into new patterns.

6. *Strive to get to the depths of problems and to acquire complete orientation in a field so that no significant factor is omitted.*

Young people with a flare for writing sometimes try to express themselves with nothing more worthy than themselves to express. It takes more than a study of journalism to write a good magazine article. It takes more than a study of methods to write a good Bible lesson. Writers must go broader and deeper than their readers, some of whom have had concentrated personal experiences in certain areas of the problem, some in other areas. Omission of one important factor will invalidate the conclusion. Readers too will bring to the material various kinds of perspective. Writers should ask themselves whether they have considered the question from the viewpoint of the large and the small, the rich and the poor, the spiritual and the carnal, the bound and the free. Modern life is no longer provincial, but a complex of interacting forces—personal, religious, cultural, economic, political, recreational.

7. Be ready to pay the price of genuine productivity—perspiration as well as inspiration.

Though vision may be high and compelling, it is seldom enough to carry a leader through to the completion of a project unless he has disciplined himself to hard work. "Too often we fail to recognize opportunity because it comes dressed in overalls and looks like work." Any creative work is one percent inspiration, ninety-nine percent perspiration. If we enjoy the activity for its own sake, we are fortunate. But who likes to redo, refine, repractice, retake?

The vision is carried out by grubby grit and grind, daily toil and struggle. It takes form only by dint of much attention to details and routine. How many of us have acquired the habit of sticking with our visions until we are sure that the Lord has done through us the best that is possible? In this day of expanding horizons it is difficult to concentrate on one skill until it is perfected.

8. Be both yielded and courageous, alert and relaxed.

". . . the people that do know their God shall be strong, and do exploits" (Daniel 11:32). Like Caleb of old they will wholly follow the Lord and not be afraid of the giants of the land to which He is directing them (Numbers 14:6–9,24). They will be humbly submissive to His leading, yet actively forging ahead on His conquests. Only those whose inner beings rest secure in the Lord will be ready to take the risks involved in all new ventures. He who is a faithful follower of God may be a leader among men.

Seldom is a leader who pioneers into the unknown approved by all the people. The natural tendency of people is to maintain the status quo, to resist change, to resent new ideas that they themselves haven't initiated. Only solid grounding in robust holiness and rugged spiritual reality will keep the leader from being poisoned by doubt or fear. He may be humbly cautious lest he offend or disrupt unnecessarily, yet cognizant of the fact that some will probably criticize. If he is sure of the call and commission of the Almighty, he can leave to Him the reactions of men.

CREATIVE CHRISTIAN TEACHING

When we go adventuring with the Creator, we may expect higher and deeper experiences than we've ever known before. Nothing is more exciting than interacting with growing personalities. Most artists and musicians transfer their dreams to inanimate canvas or clay or marble, or to a wooden or metal instrument; the medium with which teachers work is life—current life as it is being lived. Writers transcribe their ideals on paper; teachers may impress theirs on the fleshly tables of hearts.

True Christian teaching is by its very nature creative. If we are to teach pupils the Word of God rather than preach at them, we have to relate the unchanging Word to people who are always changing. We never know just what to expect. If a teaching situation is natural and normal, it is spontaneous. A boy who reacts in one way today may respond quite differently tomorrow. If we seek to get the Word inside the pupil by stimulating him to act on it, we'll have to use the part of the Bible that meets his current needs. This precludes any stereotyped, slavish conformity to a lesson plan, whether it has been prepared by the writer of a manual or by the teacher himself.

1. *The first step in Christian teaching is to prepare ourselves spiritually.*

The young teacher is often too wrapped up in himself to be free in the Lord. Yet in order to teach others, we must be in vital union with Christ and be filled with the Word and the Spirit. We must live in the part of the Word we teach until it becomes a living part of ourselves, until it is being worked out practically in our own everyday lives. Only then are we free to listen to and respond to others. Only then can we use the Word flexibly in relation to the spontaneous demands of our class.

The hardest part of creative teaching is getting started. Just as Christian character is a developmental process, so we mature progressively in teaching ability. But we will never reach our goal if we don't start out in that direction. To set our face like a flint toward that goal is to reach it some day. To start in another direction is to practice bad habits that must be overcome before the right ones can be formed.

Let the young teacher strive for the informal, conversational style that we observed in the gospel records. Can't we try to teach in the same spirit as if we were sharing an excursion with a group of friends? Our trip is a subject that the group has asked about, just as an excursion into the Word of God should be a subject the class wants to know about. In an informal group of our friends we don't do all the talking. We describe and explain what they ask about. Members of the group share similar experiences. We show pictures and objects that we brought back from the trip because they'd rather see and examine for themselves than merely listen to our words. It's not hard for us to respond to their comments because the whole trip is very vivid to us —we've lived through it. We are not bound to the strict sequence of events just as they happened; we wouldn't forget our transitions if the first question pertained to the end of the trip. The experience is exhilarating, not wearing, because we enjoy sharing what has been pleasant and profitable to us.

That should be the spirit of a Bible school session. We've had a thrilling experience with the Lord through the words of His Revelation, and we're eager to share them with our class. If their Bible study is going to lead them into their own individual experiences with the Lord, they must become actively involved so that they take unto themselves personally that portion of Scripture. In order to do that, we must start where they are, right now.

2. If several possibilities are pondered, the teacher is freer to follow the lead of the pupils.

When we sit in our room at home preparing our Bible school lesson for the next week, how do we know what our class will be ready for next Sunday? If we are not content to "just teach the Bible," and realize that we teach it to a certain few people, unlike any other people, how can we adequately prepare?

We don't know what will be their physical condition at the moment of the lesson, their mental outlook, particular psychological needs, urgent spiritual needs, and distinctive individual interests. Of course it is our business to find out just as much as possible about the typical characteristics of the age group and the personal life of the individuals in the class. And we can keep in touch with them during the week to see whether crisis or routine transpires there. But what approach can we use to penetrate to a vulnerable spot inside, to spark a problem that they've been grappling with, to make them sit on the edge of their chairs?

As we sit before the Lord with the members of our class upon our heart, we can use sanctified imagination to try to visualize what would challenge them this week. What problem would be connected in their minds with the fire that razed a factory building? What might be the implications for them of the political election? How can we lead from a newspaper item of a girl who ran away into the Bible lesson for the day? How can they learn from the defeat of the high school basketball team? What are their felt needs if life is growing rather monotonous?

If we teachers think through two or three approaches, we

won't get rutted into seeing only one possibility. If we have considered more than one, it will be easier for us to substitute yet another on the spur of the moment when some pupil makes a comment that leads right into the Bible content. One of the greatest weaknesses of young teachers— it should be repeated—is that they miss many of the best leads given by the group. They're concentrating so hard on content that they don't even hear relevant remarks.

3. *Because pupils are full of surprises, we should always be ready to shift gears, moving flexibly toward our goals.*

Once we get the conviction that we are teaching the Bible to people, we'll be sensitive as to whether or not the people are learning, and we'll change our tactics when they cease to learn—and to learn what we intend to teach, not something else of their own choosing. It often happens that as we follow through the plans that we've prepared, suddenly a member of the class gets an insight that lights up his whole being and proves contagious. As he explains what he sees, we realize that he has spurted ahead, covering in a moment several steps that we had planned. We can't usually count on that insight being gained so fast. We send up a quick "thank You" to the Lord, help the others catch up with the one who has caught the gleam, and go right on from there. As a result we may conclude the session on a different note from the one we had in mind, but oh, how much more valuable! And how much more lasting because the insight was their very own!

On the other hand, it sometimes happens that the class goes slower than we had anticipated. They are not ready to take the steps that we had outlined. We may have assumed that they have had content or experiences which are necessary as a basis for the present study when in reality this background is lacking. There may be a block that we have to pause to remove, either a mental or an emotional or a moral block. It may require the rest of the hour to remove that block, but what would be the profit of trying to continue as planned if the pupils weren't with us? Too often teachers aren't aware of whether or not the group is with them. They go blithely on their own way, leaving the pupils to their own devices.

The hallmark of the mature teacher is his skill in meeting the pupils where they are, and going forward as fast as they are able to go, guiding them in the use of content that meets whatever need arises in the process.

4. *Though Christian content is authoritative, the pupils determine the selection of content, its order, speed, details.*

While the answers to all our problems, or at least the principles, are to be found in God's written Revelation of Himself rather than in any human source, which problems we shall discuss, in what order, with what speed, to what extent, depend upon the pupils who must appropriate the answers. At the teacher's disposal is the whole library of inscripturated books—various types of literature, from various eras, written by various types of personalities. For each problem at each age level the teacher should know which part of Scripture best meets that need in terms of the experience of the group.

Bible content for young children is organized in terms of personal themes, with several lessons stressing that same theme from different angles. Juniors for the first time can appreciate history and geography, so their lessons take them chronologically through the active hero stories of the Bible, omitting the abstract. Junior Highs need practical studies to relieve their doubts and fears. In addition to the Christian life, Seniors usually need a rapid survey of the whole Bible, integrating the fragmentary bits that they have gleaned through the years. Young people need the doctrines brought together from all parts of Scripture, and adults study systematic theology in relation to basic philosophical questions.

For children one Scriptural incident is enough for one Bible story and one session; more than that would confuse rather than enlighten. The details that are close to their experience are included, others are omitted lest they get a distorted view of God's ways. Under supervision young people are able to trace trends, to discover relationships, and determine the reasons for the inclusion or omission of details in Scripture. Adults should be able to abstract and generalize the essence of truth from the various types of literature.

5. *The Spirit helps the teacher determine when to declare truth, when to guide the pupils in discovering the truth for themselves.*

One of the most delicate skills of the teacher is to know when to declare and when to guide. If we only declared or spoke the truth, the pupils would not become actively involved in the process. If we only guided them in seeking for themselves, we would sometimes waste precious time, for sometimes they are ready to be told. When they are already motivated, when there isn't time to lead them through the slower process of exploring for themselves, Christian teachers do not hesitate to explain eternal truth. Because it is usually easier and more natural for the teacher to declare, we ought to take pains to perfect the art of guidance. The divine Teacher is always ready to lead us in the choice of method.

6. *A variety of methods suggest themselves as the teacher seeks to help the pupils make the outer spiritual factors their own.*

It is a pity when a teacher overuses a few methods when many others would better accomplish his purposes as well as add the spice of variety. Whenever a need arises, we ought to ask, "How can we best meet this particular situation?" instead of asking "Can I find a story or a flannelgraph to use now?"

As we study the intrinsic nature of the content, new possibilities open up to us. Interesting combinations of content make for fascinating new patterns of thought. Applying the Word of God to new situations ought to result in fresh ideas. Just as we expect our pupils to create original forms without copying the patterns of others, so we should be continually using new combinations of methods—drawing, models, illustrations of principles, posters, maps, creative writing of prose and poetry, discussion, role playing, skits, debate, reports, composing music, adapting music, games, tests, interviews, research, trips, observations, collections, time lines, planning worship services, choral reading, etc.

The following comments are typical of the creative teacher who stimulates originality:

That's your problem, not mine.
Are you satisfied with that?
Ask Wayne—he's an authority on that.
What do *you* think?
What are *you* doing about it?
Where did you look to try to find the answer?
Looks as if it were done by a machine, but it doesn't look like your idea.

VIII

STRUCTURING THE CURRICULUM

The transition from Scriptural foundations to actual teaching practice is bridged by the curriculum. Scriptural principles are implemented by the outlining of cycles and series of lessons, which are broken up into individual lessons. The word *curriculum* literally means a "racecourse." Traditionally the course was considered the *body of content* that the student covered in his educational progress. More recently the term connotes the *activity of the student* as he runs through various experiences which involve content.

In a Scriptural orientation the "curriculum" may be defined as those activities in relation to authoritative content that are guided or employed by Christian leadership in order to bring pupils one step nearer to maturity in Christ. These activities imply interaction of both teachers and pupils with the Word of God. Because learning, as previously defined, is an active, inner, on-going, disciplined process, the teacher does nothing that the pupils can more profitably do themselves.

211

THE CENTER OF THE CURRICULUM

The most crucial question in structuring a curriculum is the question of its center. Do not all Christians agree that both authoritative content and personal experience are essential if pupils are to appropriate for themselves the full salvation that is offered to them in Christ? Neither factor of the curriculum, content, or experience, can be omitted or minimized with impunity. But one of them must constitute the center around which the other revolves, the source of authority upon which the other depends as a secondary element.

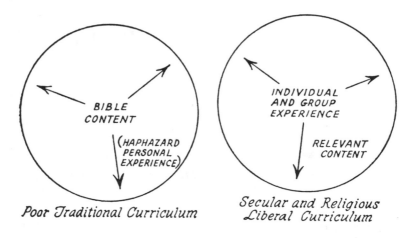

Poor Traditional Curriculum   *Secular and Religious Liberal Curriculum*

In poor traditional Christian education the content of the Bible was the whole curriculum. Bible facts were diligently studied by the teacher and given out to pupils, who were expected to absorb them mentally, to memorize them, and then automatically to apply them. The experience which resulted from the teaching of these facts was haphazard. Sometimes pupils were sufficiently motivated to practice them, sometimes they saw the relationship between these facts and their own daily lives, but these connections between the Bible and life were not an integral part of the lesson. Sometimes also the pupils got through the printed words on paper and the factual data of Scripture to have personal dealings with the Lord, but often they did not. Many are the young people who have been exposed to enough factual Scripture to enable them to live deeply spiritual lives, yet they have not actively inwardly appropriated the truth that they understand mentally.

At the other extreme is the secular and religious liberal curriculum that is centered in experience. Since it is the pupil who must do the growing, who must accept the content, he is given priority in the school's activities. As the pupils' needs are met, as they are motivated to interact with content that meets their needs, they originate and reorganize relevant content and bring it to life. The advocates of experience-centered systems assert that no curriculum that is centered in content can be dynamic, only the ones that are centered in life. Only as pupils search and find the content that has a bearing on current life will it enrich and change life.

What is the truth in this outlook? What the weakness? Can Christians accomplish their aims in a structure that is man-centered? No, only a God-centered curriculum can be Christian. Can we put the Word of God in the center and yet have a dynamic curriculum? We can, for no other book is comparable to God's Revelation. God means His words to be more than facts, even eternal facts. He means them to reveal Himself and His Son. He never meant us to separate the written Word from the Living Word. The Living Word is contacted only through the written record. Therefore Christians have a curriculum that is Word-centered rather than Bible-centered.

And lo, what an amazing thing we have now! A curriculum that is centered not in sinful human life, but in divine Life Himself, eternal life, fulness of life, the Living Word revealed by the written Word! What center can compare with that for vitality and power!

But experience with the Word cannot be left to chance. It will not automatically proceed from the written Word. Teachers must make definite provision for including experience in the curriculum. Though not the center of the Christian structure, experience is necessary because:

The aim of Christian education is maturity in Christ to the glory of God.

The Word must be personally, actively appropriated.

Knowledge alone is not power, but the effective use of knowledge.

Experience is the best teacher if it is guided by the Word.

Factual content alone is only theory, sterile verbalism.

Therefore experience occupies an essential though secondary place in the Christian curriculum. The Word of God is originally an outer factor, external to the learning pupil. But as the divine and human teachers stimulate interaction between the Word and the pupil, both written and Living Word gradually or suddenly penetrate to the interior of the pupil. It is the peculiar ministry of the Holy Spirit to make the outer Word an inner experience, for He operates both without and within. As the outer Word becomes experience, there is progressively less of the self-life and more of the Christ-life until the Lord Himself becomes the controlling factor in the whole of life. Maturity in Christ consists of the Word's becoming our experience, becoming our life.

The divine Teacher, with the cooperation of the human teacher, leads the pupil from his current need into the Word, where he gains new insight into truth, then out again to practice the Word in daily life situations. The pupil's experience impels him to seek knowledge of the Word, which in turn commands him to return to life to practice the truth. The real test is the amalgamation of inner and outer forces until it is difficult to separate them. The Word becomes flesh, and our mortal bodies reflect the Word.

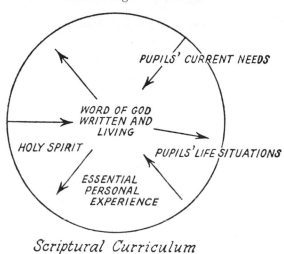

Scriptural Curriculum

How tremendous would be the results if all Bible teaching would set in motion these earth-shaking forces!

DEVELOPING A UNIT OF WORK

Whenever a new series of lessons is projected or a series in current use fails to meet specific needs, how do teachers or writers proceed to set up the type of interaction that has just been described? All leaders need to understand curriculum structure, for they will use it even in adapting printed materials, and who does not need to do that? Who can expect to find ready-prepared lessons that are tailored to fit individual groups? Major publishing houses must meet typical needs, and whose needs are typical?

When all the principles discussed in this book are brought to bear upon the problems of curriculum, the result is a unit of work. The ministry of Christ on earth may be divided into two main curriculum units: the early part of His life up to Peter's confession of His deity, which was the culminating activity of the first unit; then the latter part of His life culminating in His death, resurrection, and ascension. The focal problem of the first unit is "Who am I?" Of the second, "What did I come to do?" The events within these two major units naturally fall into minor units, some of which are most naturally expressed in terms of content, as "the nature of the Kingdom"; and some in terms of experience, as "faith."

A unit of work may be defined as the organization of teaching-learning situations around a central core, a focal problem, that integrates both content and experience for the learner. A unit may be a long-term project, lasting a year or two, or a short-term project consisting of three or four lessons.

There are many reasons for organizing curriculum materials into units of work. Units emphasize learning rather than teaching, thus stimulating new pupil experiences with content when it is more natural for teachers to stress content at the expense of experience. Units afford continuity both of content and experience. Especially in Christian agencies which hold sessions lasting only one hour a week, with seven days between, is it difficult for pupils to appreciate the relationship between separate lessons. If long-range goals are sighted and plans are made for reaching them, each discrete activity is seen in the light of the whole rather than as a fragmentary bit. Then motivation is stronger, integration surer. It is easier for both teachers and pupils to be flexible in revising plans to keep up with changing needs. When the content is connected with current life, it is either used or made ready to use as an integral part of the unit.

It is not to be expected that units of work developed for one agency will take the same form as those developed for other agencies. For instance, the curriculum outlined for Sunday school, one hour a week, looks quite different from a camping curriculum that runs every hour, consecutively, for two weeks. Likewise, a curriculum planned for young children who cannot read and who have little foresight will appear quite different from one planned for young people who can do independent research and committee work. What does remain the same under all circumstances is the underlying spirit of a unit of work, the spirit of quest and adventure and discovery, in which pupils seek and find new things in the Lord, in which they identify their own needs and meet them in Christ.

THE TEACHER'S PREPLANNING

Putting emphasis on the pupils' learning rather than the teacher's teaching doesn't mean that we teachers are less important or that we'll have less to do. It probably means that we'll have more to do. As followers of John Amos Comenius, who first enunciated this emphasis, we plan and prepare in relation to our pupils as well as our content. We must experientially know both pupils and content. Formerly content was sufficient.

First we pray through and study thoroughly the needs, interests, capacities of our particular group in the light of the Word of God. On the basis of these needs we formulate general and specific aims. The general aims we keep in the back of our minds, glad when we see gradual progress along those lines. The specific aims we keep written large upon our hearts, relating everything that happens to them. If possible, the outstanding objective should be stated in a single, short sentence or phrase so that our focus is not blurred. This aim is best stated in terms of new conduct, attitudes, skill or knowledge, often in terms of a change in conduct which also involves attitudes, skills, and knowledge.

We then select general and specific areas of essential content that meet these needs. The needs will be met by the written Word of God which leads to the Living Word, but not by just any part of the written Word. Teachers ought

to be ready to suggest that part of the Bible that is closest
to the problematical life situation, whose characters have
most in common with our life today. James 1:21 uses the
figure of the engrafted Word, the inserting of a fruitful
shoot into wild natural stock until a permanent union is
effected. The closer the Scripture is to life today, the easier
will be the union.

Next we saturate ourselves with this part of God's Word
until we are wholly absorbed with it. Until we feel it,
breathe it, live it, dream it. Until we are completely at home
with its implications. Until we are so filled with its possibilities for our own class that we are bursting to do something
about it. Then we are ready to lead our pupils to that same
vision and action. Then we can be free and flexible in our
use of this eternal truth with pupils who are full of surprises.

The next step is to visualize various types of intrinsic
motivation. Probably the most important single factor in
the success of a unit of work is the enthusiasm with which
it is launched. If it gets off to a running start, this push-off
gathers enough momentum to carry it a long way. Otherwise feet will drag and interest lag. Even if an adequate
launching should take a whole hour or more, it is time well
spent, for the planning in itself is an educational experience. Planning requires the selection of past experience
and content, insight into relationships between past and
future, judgment as to possible procedures.

In terms of all we know and can discover about the members of our group, we find the points where the content
areas touch their current lives and make a difference in
what they want to do here and now. What is the connection
between their felt needs and God's answers? It may be that
we'll need to lead into their real spiritual needs as a second
step rather than the first, if to begin there would leave
them cold. No matter how far away from the final goal we
have to start, the takeoff must be where they are right

now or they won't move toward the goal. It won't help
them at all for us leaders to take the trip without them.
It must be their unit, their progress, their values, their
work.

Intrinsic motivation taps the pupils' inner drives and
urges that the Lord God has put within all of us. It holds
out something that is worth knowing and doing for its own
sake. Even if the present level of motivation is rather low
because higher levels as yet hold no appeal, even if the
pupils see no connection between spiritual standards and
their own daily life, still we must get them in touch with
spiritual Reality at a low level rather than train them to seek
selfish ends.

Extrinsic motivation implies that spiritual life is not
worth seeking for its own sake. It holds out to pupils irrelevant prizes or rewards that have nothing to do with the
major thrust of the unit. It implies that studying the Bible
is an unpleasant task which requires sugarcoating to make
it palatable. Nothing is more important in the Christian life
than motives. We want our young people to desire the Lord
first of all for Himself—nothing is more attractive than He
is—and to desire the things of the Lord because they satisfy
the inmost longings of the soul. They must experience the
joy of fellowship with Him before He can trust them with
His gifts or His service.

Therefore we'll bestir ourselves to create a setting which
will arouse thought and questions along the line of the unit.
For children this setting may be effected by large objects
that they can manipulate, pictures that they can discuss,
trips that afford new experience. For young people and
adults we can steer informal conversation to questions in
a given area, we can write thought-provoking questions on
the chalkboard, we can espouse experiments and new projects that they show interest in. The best leads are always
those that arise naturally out of the pupils' daily grappling
with their own daily life situations.

PLANNING WITH THE PUPILS

If a unit of work is to be the pupils' rather than the teacher's, if they are to become actively involved so that they do the learning, they must share in the planning. If we leaders have previously prepared ourselves to lead them, they won't flounder and waste time, for we have already envisaged some of the possibilities that will work and some that won't be practical. But if we are true leaders rather than dictators, we're ready to let go our plans if the pupils come up with something better. They may prefer to adopt a plan we have conceived rather than anything they originate. That is perfectly legitimate, just so they wholeheartedly accept it.

But they must shoulder the problem. If they feel that it is ours rather than theirs, they'll let us carry it, and then we'll get the benefit, not they. Only if it is their problem, will they keep it on their hearts and assume responsibility for its solution.

It is often practical to write on a chalkboard what the pupils already know about the problem, and what they would like to find out. These areas are then organized and broken up into subproblems, and the order of attack decided upon. It may be that the whole group will want to work on the whole problem, or the group may divide into committees that each take one aspect. If committees are used, it is well to have a natural leader in each group.

The main purpose and subsidiary purposes should be clarified very specifically so that the pupils know exactly what they're looking for in God's Word and just how they will go about it. This planning should be much more detailed than it usually is.

It is not to be assumed that this initial planning will be followed rigidly to the end of the unit. As the group gets into the content, new insight and new background will often necessitate a change of plans if real needs are to be met. Continual evaluation is an integral part of the process. At intervals the students pause to see how far they have come, and to revise plans for the future. As the teacher helps them solve their felt needs, he tries to go on to help them sense and meet their real spiritual needs.

FINDING THE ANSWERS

If the problems are the pupils' own and they see clearly how to attack them, they will be ready to mobilize their energies in finding the answers. Many types of activity will be included in most units, most of them requiring thought and judgment rather than listening and rote memorization. The pupils will continually be selecting content that is relevant to their problem, judging its value, organizing data, finding new leads, sharing their findings with others, evaluating the validity of their conclusions, and checking results. The genuine personal satisfaction they derive from reaching the solution is their best reward. They will be more ready to practice truth that they themselves have discovered.

As the pupils work, the teacher supervises, providing further motivation should interest lag, suggesting new approaches or sources, helping to organize and evaluate what is found. The teacher's business is to keep the pupils working profitably and to help them appreciate the significance of what they find.

Of course the first specific method is always research in Scripture for pupils who can read, listening to a Bible story for those who cannot read. Young people need to realize that the answers to their practical questions are found in Scripture if they only know where to look and how to translate Hebrew customs and problems in terms of current living. The teacher guides them in making concrete factual observations of what the Bible actually says before they try to interpret what it means for them. They form the habit of depending upon the illumination of the Holy Spirit, of comparing Scripture with Scripture, of sharpening their intellectual perception.

Supplementing Bible study will be the use of versions, concordances, Bible dictionaries, atlases, commentaries, notes on manners and customs, and pictures. In order to learn how Biblical principles are implemented in our day, the pupils may interview the Lord's people, make surveys, send questionnaires, write letters, visit churches and missions and museums, study architecture, make collections, illustrate Scripture and hymns. Whenever possible, direct experience should be substituted for vicarious experience with words.

The teacher should be flexible enough to substitute another phase of essential content for the one he had planned in order to meet each response as it arises, but should do this without disrupting the overall curriculum. If he feels led, or time and circumstances do not permit pupil activity, he does not hesitate to give direct instruction that meets the needs.

CULMINATING ACTIVITY

A curriculum unit is brought to the most satisfying conclusion when some type of activity ties the whole process together and if possible makes use of the main findings. Every curriculum should end in practice of the truth, or at least in visualization of the difference that truth ought to make in daily life. Unless our pupils can use the new truth in new situations, it is not really their own, and they will soon forget it.

A common example of culminating activity is the closing demonstration of a Vacation Bible School when the pupils share with their parents and friends what they've been doing during the school. This program introduces nothing new and extraneous, but selects the most interesting things from the regular schedule. If the demonstration includes spiritual progress as well as factual material, it can be of great value to the pupils themselves as well as to their guests. It sharply focuses the main purpose of the school and aids the transfer of Scripture to daily life.

The culminating activity may take a variety of forms. One may be the organization of findings into a chart or outline or time line. Since all groups need organization of content insofar as the age level is able to appreciate it, the whole should be viewed at the end as well as at the beginning. In a functional review the main thrust of a unit stands out more clearly, with the significance of each part seen in relation to the whole. The best way to review is to use.

If committees are working on several aspects of a problem, they may plan interesting ways of presenting their reports to the other groups, and then all may formulate a summary of the whole. If group members have gained new insights into spiritual life, they may use them to lead a worship service for another group. They may show what they have gained by constructing a work of art or a mural or a model, or by the creative writing of a magazine article, a letter, a report to the church, a story, tract, or skit. Some units are of such a nature that their natural outgrowth is a service project, such as building a playground for children, decorating a room at church, collecting papers to sell, weeding a garden, or putting on a banquet in appreciation for the work of others.

During all the steps of a curriculum unit the teacher should keep on the lookout for leading-on values. Does this study motivate the group to study a related question? Did relevant questions arise that could not be incorporated into this unit, but which the group showed real enthusiasm for? When once our Bible teaching comes to grips with real life as it is being currently lived, we won't need artificial stimulation; we'll be alert to new needs as they arise and start our teaching there.

AN EXAMPLE OF A CURRICULUM UNIT

For a brief illustration of a unit of work, let's take a series of Sunday school lessons on the subject of the Holy Spirit for Junior High young people. We as teachers open a new manual to the first unit of five lessons:

> The Holy Spirit as Teacher and Guide
> The Holy Spirit as Counselor
> The Holy Spirit as Illuminator
> The Holy Spirit as Enabler
> The Holy Spirit as Convicter.

First we survey the work for the whole quarter and the place of this unit in the whole. We ask ourselves whether or not our particular class needs this emphasis, and we immediately answer with assurance, "It surely does." Therefore we bow before the Lord with the names of our pupils on our hearts, asking Him to do His gracious inner work in each one, listing the specific things that need to be done in each life in relation to the Holy Spirit.

"Dear Lord, help Jack to see that You are real, that You seek to speak personally to him by Your Spirit through the Word, that You can answer his doubts and fears."

"Help Joan to find You as her best Pal, who can supply her emotional needs by Your Spirit, and stabilize her life."

We then concentrate on the Scriptures that describe the person and work of the Holy Spirit until they have become so much a part of our thinking that we can turn readily from one passage to another. We apply all that we study to ourselves and ask the Spirit to give us new experiences with the Word. We also ask our divine indwelling Teacher to show us how the content of these five lessons can meet the specific needs of the class. Which part of this unit is closest to Jack's needs? Which to Joan's? As we study we are prompted by that same Holy Spirit to pray again that these truths may penetrate deep into consciousness and do a searching work in each life.

But we've been thinking of this new unit even before we make definite preparation to teach it. Even last quarter we were looking ahead in order to motivate it. When reference to God's Spirit was made in the study of the last topic, we took a minute to ask a few personal questions about the Holy Spirit. If the group responded by commenting or asking further questions, we'd pause to whet its appetite for this study, remarking that we ought to have a study of the Spirit in the future.

When the young people enter their classroom on the first day of the new unit, they find written on the chalkboard these questions:

Do you know a Christian who is filled with the Spirit of God? Why do you think he is?
Is the Spirit-filled Christian long-faced and serious?
Is there anything spooky connected with the Spirit?
Are young people ever filled with the Spirit? If so, do they die young?
What questions do you have about the Spirit?

These very frank questions will undoubtedly get the group thinking about the subject as soon as they arrive. If you are there early, ready to use their comments, you can stimulate further questions that reveal individual concerns. You can write their questions on another chalkboard panel, and on still another write what they already know about the Holy Spirit. They will surely be bored if you begin to teach what they already know. But they'll be alert to discover the answers to their own questions.

If you have studied all five lessons in the series, you won't need to begin with the first one, or to keep arbitrary lines between the various ministries of the Spirit. You'll be able to begin with whichever problem seems most urgent and most introductory for your particular pupils as the Spirit enables you to sense their needs. You can begin at once to help them find their answers in Scripture and to discuss the practical implications to their own lives. You won't need to *tell* them the answers because they'll be turning the pages of their Bibles until they locate a passage that speaks to them personally. If they have prepared an assignment for today, that background will facilitate the search for answers to these new questions. You will act as stimulator and guide to make sure they see valid relationships and interpretations. The class period will find the pupils busily engaged in exploring their own Bibles and making their own applications.

The next four Sundays will be a continuation of this teaching-learning process. Each session will normally raise as well as answer several questions about the Holy Spirit. At the end of each session the pupils should have a personal problem to study and pray about during the week, a practical problem dealing with what the Spirit seeks to do in their lives or just how He can help them.

Each week when they leave class they should also have one definite truth in relation to the Spirit to act upon during the week. It might be His wisdom in difficult decisions, it might be His power in avoiding temptation and overcoming self, it might be His conviction of sin as they pray for a loved one. In presession the following Sunday they are encouraged to discuss how the Spirit aided them during the week. This discussion will keep the study realistic and down-to-earth.

Another way to demonstrate the dynamic reality of the Spirit today is to suggest that young people interview mature respected members of the church who radiate the fulness of Christ. They may like to ask how the Holy Spirit operates under certain conditions that they are curious about. Advanced pupils may like to read and report on parts of books that describe how the Spirit moved young people like Hudson Taylor of the China Inland Mission and

William Borden of Yale. Assuredly the presence of the Spirit should be felt in the group as He supplies the teacher with supernatural insight and enables the pupils to appropriate the Word.

Near the end of the unit the teacher is watching for cues that would lead to a profitable culminating activity. If Joan remarks that her sister needs the help of the Holy Spirit, the teacher might comment that the class could plan and conduct a worship service when they could share with Joan's sister's class the impact of what they have been learning. If the pastor of another evangelical church in town happens to be preaching Sunday evening on this subject, they might attend in a group and enjoy a snack at teacher's house afterward. They might like to summarize their study by making a list of Bible references that would help them when they don't know what decision to make, when they feel discouraged, when they feel lonely, and so forth. Some groups enjoy making a list of fallacies about the Holy Spirit and posting it on the church bulletin board. If we teachers are sensitive to cues that the pupils give, and if we habitually make the most of such suggestions, they will often propose good ideas themselves.

CRITERIA FOR EVALUATING PRINTED MATERIALS

Since a rare combination of insight and skill is required before a teacher is qualified to prepare his own Bible lessons, most of us are glad to leave that task to experts who are professionally trained. But each church is responsible for selecting the series of lessons that comes closest to meeting its local needs. Sad to say, the selection is often made on the basis of how easy the lessons are to teach or how colorful the jacket is.

What teachers should look for in printed manuals is the extent to which the writers help them apply Scriptural principles to the local situation. Local teachers in all kinds of schools in all parts of the country need material that achieves a delicate balance between specificity and flexibility. If suggestions are not definite and practical, teachers fail to get clear-cut ideas of teaching procedures, for generalizations and abstractions are not readily translated into action. If suggestions are not flexible, teachers are inclined to follow the manual slavishly without making connections with their own classes.

The Scriptural principles explained in this book work out in the following criteria for evaluating printed materials:

I. Use of Content
   A. Is the Bible regarded as the objective, propositional Word of God, the infallible guide to faith and practice, the source of authority?
   B. Is the curriculum centered in the Word of God—the written record revealing the Living Word?
   C. Does the content emphasize Biblical essentials: regeneration, growth in grace, service?
   D. Are the Biblical facts used in an accurate and forceful manner?
   E. Is the extra-Biblical content true to Scriptural principles and introduced for the purpose of making the Bible relevant to daily life?
   F. Is the whole curriculum unified and comprehensive, with each part properly integrated in the whole? It is comprehensive if it attains the nine ultimate aims of Christian education: right relation to God the Father, Son, the Holy Spirit; knowledge and love and practical use of the Bible; formulation of a Christian world and life view; a progressively closer walk with Christ; assuming of responsibility in the church, for the lost everywhere, and in the civic community.
II. Use of Experience
   A. Is the individual helped to grow continually and to take definite steps toward balanced maturity in Christ?
   B. Is provision made for major and minor decisions so that the pupils develop their own personal convictions?

    C. Is provision made for pupil purposing, the solution of vital problems, and the carrying out of ideas?

    D. Are the pupils' personal, immediate experiences used whenever possible rather than vicarious experiences?

    E. Does the curriculum stress the essential elements in the pupils' experience and minimize the less essential (spiritual progress primarily; mental, psychological, social, physical, secondarily)?

III. Relation of Content and Experience

    A. Is the Bible used functionally to produce changes in pupils rather than as an end in itself?

    B. Is the material selected and graded to meet the present interests, needs, and capacities of the average pupil at the various age levels?

    C. Does the curriculum make provision for meeting the needs of home, church, secular school, and community?

IV. Meeting the Needs of the Pupil

    A. Does the material appeal to and challenge the individual?

    B. In the activities suggested for pupils, is provision made for individual differences—between pupils, classes, geographical areas, and so forth?

    C. Are the psychological needs of the individual met: freedom from guilt, security, affection, recognition, new experiences?

V. Meeting the Needs of the Teacher

    A. Is the material self-explanatory, practical, definite?

    B. Is the material flexible enough to meet the needs of large and small churches, trained and untrained teachers, pupils with diverse backgrounds, diverse geographical areas?

    C. Is the general tone of the material one of spiritual warmth, vitality, challenge?

    D. Does the curriculum provide inspiration, Biblical background, and teaching principles in addition to definite suggestions for lessons?

    E. Does it guide the teacher in using life situations of his own pupils to make the Bible real to them?

VI.   Meeting the Needs of the Agency
    A. Does the curriculum take advantage of the distinctive needs and possibilities of the agency for which it is prepared? (For the Sunday school: primarily instruction and worship; for the Vacation Bible School: all four elements of instruction, worship, expression, fellowship, and so forth.)

VII. Mechanical Features of Printed Materials
    A. Do the high quality and standards of the material reflect its eternal values?
    B. Is the material printed in a manner that facilitates teaching and learning: layout, type, binding, vocabulary, illustrations?

USING PRINTED LESSON MATERIALS

Even after a school has selected the series of lessons that comes closest to meeting its particular needs, it must expect to adapt that series to local conditions. Not because the series has weaknesses as printed curriculum, but of necessity it has to be written for typical teachers and typical pupils in typical situations. And those situations exist only in educational textbooks. This does not imply lack of respect for lesson writers, who should be professionally trained in age-group methods. The local teacher should try to find the reason why the manual suggests everything that is in it. Lesson writers have reasons that local groups aren't always aware of and that should be discovered before teachers dismiss them summarily as inappropriate.

But the most expert of writers can't write for any one church. Therefore teachers must know what in their manuals they should expect to adapt, and how. If teachers first of all sit before the Lord with the needs of their own pupils upon their hearts, they will be in a mood for picking up their manual and relating all they read to their own class. Nothing will take the place of preliminary prayer, which focuses the personal needs of the pupils in the light of the Father's best for them.

LONG-RANGE PLANNING

A teacher should then read the whole manual, absorbing the perspective and flavor of the whole quarter. As he reads, he evaluates in terms of his own class. Does the spirit of the whole meet the needs of my pupils? Should they be different people after studying these lessons? Do the aims seem to be pointed directly at them—deeply, personally? Would a slight change of focus do more for them? Is each lesson needed by them, or is there one aspect of the whole that is most urgently needed? Can I strengthen this emphasis without destroying the continuity of the series? Might it be wise to revamp a lesson or two in order to stress the needed emphasis?

If a teacher has previewed the whole quarter, he will be able to teach pupils more flexibly within that framework. If a pupil is bothered today about a question that comes in a later lesson, it might be wise to take that lesson today rather than to put him off until later when he may have lost all interest in the subject. A pupil's readiness for a subject counts more than its logical organization, though that should follow if interest is retained. If we are ready to suggest Scripture that answers a pupil's question, we are often able to incorporate it into the day's lesson without switching subjects. Such is the richness of God's Word that a given passage often teaches more than one principle and may without distortion be approached from more than one angle.

PARTICULARIZING THE APPROACH

When teachers read the lesson approach that is printed in their manual, they should ask themselves:

Will this approach make my pupils sit on the edge of their chairs?
Is this a problem with which they're vitally concerned?
How much momentum will this approach gain for the lesson?

At times teachers will be satisfied that the approach suggested in the manual is the best possible beginning for the lesson. At other times the printed approach would no doubt leave a particular class cold.

Teachers will then ask themselves these questions as they conjure up in their mind's eye their own Harry and Ann:

How can their personal world be tapped to lead into the Bible content?

Where does this truth touch their daily lives?

What of consequence happened to them this very week?

What may be on their minds and hearts as they come to Bible class?

The carrying power of the whole lesson will depend largely upon the approach. If the pupils get personally involved at the very beginning, they will normally search for answers, catch insights, offer suggestions, in general "push" the lesson. The process of visualizing various types of intrinsic motivation is the same as that for motivating a unit of work, which was analyzed earlier in this chapter. If more than one approach is sighted, it is easier for the teacher to discard them in favor of one that the pupils offer spontaneously at the moment, for the latter will no doubt gather up most force.

Using the Pupils' Interaction

After the approach gets the pupils initially involved, the methods used should keep them continually interacting with the Word of God, written and Living. We are not truly teaching when we lecture content regardless of what the pupils are doing and thinking. It is their interaction that determines how we proceed. They must progressively receive more and more of the written Word, which will lead them to receive more and more of the Living Word. As they themselves discover the exciting truths of the eternal world, it becomes easier for them to obey those truths.

If children have heard the day's story given in the manual, we don't proceed to tell it anyway and thereby to bore them and engender negative attitudes toward Scripture. Perhaps we ask them to tell it, or parts of it. Or read it directly from their Bibles, if they are able. When they begin to tell it, they may discover that there are many details that they don't know; then they'll be ready to look or listen for them.

In an atmosphere that encourages questions and comments and suggestions, we follow through every honest contribution. If members of the group frown or look puzzled, we find out what is behind that facial expression. If a sudden insight is gained, we may be able to spurt ahead and cover more material than is scheduled for one lesson. If pupils are not ready for a truth because they lack background, we may have to back up, add supplementary material, and slow down.

When someone asks a question that seems irrelevant, we try to discover what connection the ideas had in his mind, which may be just the clue that will open up his life to the glorious Light of the world. (That is, unless he is being flippant and just trying to gain attention.) Often we must look beneath the question to the questioner, for timid souls ask factual questions to hide the real personal question that is lurking inside. It often happens that a pupil tries out the group until he finds whether or not he is accepted as a person in his own right, whether he is permitted to express what he actually feels, though it may appear heretical.

What do we do when pupils make comments such as:

I don't believe that.

Why do scholars disagree on this point?

How can we find out what the Holy Spirit wants to do in each of us?

How can I be my brother's keeper?

I could draw a picture that shows what we've been talking about.

Shouldn't we show this community that we are Christians?

Many earnest teachers never hear comments like this. Yet they are invaluable leads to the sensitive teacher, for every remark like these means that the pupils have been taking the Word unto themselves and are reacting to it. If they form the habit of making the Word personal and doing something about it, they are on their way to maturity in Christ. We don't know what they're thinking unless they tell us. We don't know how to proceed unless they show us where they are now. Why not encourage them to give illustrations of Scriptural principles instead of doing it ourselves? As pupils make suggestions for projects and activities, they will aggressively assume responsibility for carrying them out. The work will be theirs, the class theirs, the growth theirs.

Providing Opportunities for Practice

If a teacher truly believes that ". . . to him that knoweth to do good and doeth it not, to him it is sin" (James 4:17), he will not consider his Bible lesson finished when the Scriptural principles have been discovered. He will not assume that pupils will automatically obey one of God's commands because they understand it mentally. Their whole being needs to be challenged in relation to that mental insight. Their wills and emotions are harnessed by means of worship, either a planned worship service, or spontaneous worship whenever emotional feeling reaches a high point, or a brief moment of worship at the culmination of Bible study. Instruction and worship then bring pupils to the place where they are prompted to do something outwardly about the truth that they have received inwardly. Personal application should be an integral part of each lesson.

In every classroom there are opportunities for the practice of God's Word if teachers only had eyes to see them. As children work and play with relevant objects and handwork materials and visual aids, many occasions arise for sharing and cooperating and showing love. When all of them naturally want the longest pencil with the best eraser, a child can be commended when he leaves it for someone else. When several children want to move the leading figure on the flannelgraph board, they form the habit of giving in to others. They learn to take turns sitting beside their beloved teacher. When only one may perform an active service that they'd all like to do, they should connect their own selfish or unselfish acts with the Bible stories and verses that they are learning to repeat.

Young people, and adults too, can often work out the truth in their Bible classes. The over-talker will not monopolize the discussion if he projects himself into the situation of the shy member, who has problems too, who needs to be brought out of himself by others who are concerned about his spiritual growth as well as their own intersts. How many adult classes practice the precept: "Let nothing be done through strife or vainglory; but in lowliness of mind let each esteem other better than themselves. Look not every man on this own things, but every man also on the things of others" (Philippians 2:3,4)?

If teachers realize that pupils often have insights and experiences to contribute, they'll be democratic rather than dictatorial in their leadership of the group. When decisions are in the offing, they'll seek the mind of the Spirit in the group rather than trying to push through their own preferences.

Of course it isn't possible to practice in the classroom many of the truths of God's Word, because it is intended for the whole of life. But at least teachers can help their pupils visualize how the Christ-life may be lived at home and school and in work and play. They can use some of the lesson period for discussion of practical implications rather than spending the whole time on the exposition of new truth when what is already known is not being put to work. Many a Christian businessman in theory holds high moral principles that he is not putting into operation in his office or shop. He has never seen his business practices from the viewpoint of God or his employees. In a warm, personal setting he needs to see the needs of the other fellow, who looks at the office or shop from a different perspective.

If there isn't time for both an intensive study of the Word and its application, adult Bible classes sometimes decide to hold round-table discussions in homes during the week or on Sunday afternoon. For instance, a like-minded circle of Christian parents find it fascinating to ponder such questions as:

In what sense is father the head of the house?
What questions should the family council decide?
What constitutes Christian culture in the home?
How can family altar meet the current needs of various ages?
How can members of a family enjoy each other on family night at home?

Young people can spend the Sunday morning hour in the Bible, then use their Sunday evening young people's hour for discussion of its implications. Each group can decide how long and how often it wants to meet, just so this expressional part of the Christian program is not omitted.

Christians who get into the habit of being doers of the Word and not hearers only will continually be initiating group and individual projects. Why should not Christians be the first to lend a helping hand to a family in an emergency, when a home burns or when a mother is lost? When rooms in the church need redecorating, it should not be necessary to hire outsiders. If group members support wholly or partially a missionary known personally to them, they will find it harder to live in luxury and ease when their friends afar lack the necessities of life.

If our pupils begin to experience the thrill of seeing the Lord of life work through them, they'll be open to many urgent needs that will take them out of themselves and their own narrow lives.

IX

THE HUMAN TEACHER WORKING
WITH THE DIVINE TEACHER

Throughout the preceding chapters mention has often
been made of the crucial place of the Spirit of God in
education that is Christian. Most Christian teachers are
quick to acknowledge that unless the Spirit does His gracious work in the life of the pupil, our human efforts are
perfectly futile. Yet how few either in theory or practice
know how to work with the Spirit. The tendency is to go to
one of two extremes, either to leave all or nothing to Him.

Sometimes the following statement is made to try to
clarify His part and our part:

> Pray as if it all depended on God;
> work as if it all depended on you.

How helpful is this advice? Does it all depend upon God?
If it does, why isn't the world saved? Why doesn't the Al-

mighty use His infinite power to smite all His enemies with one stroke? He could easily do this. But He has chosen to limit Himself by what we will do, and to work through us, even through *us*. We cannot pray as if it all depended on God, for this is not God's will.

And surely it does not all depend on us. This fallacy is much worse than the former. For God can work in sovereign grace independent of us, though He seldom chooses to do so. If we work as if it all depends on us, we'll go on in our sterile busyness, frittering away our time and energy in the flesh to no avail. We may as well be making strenuous motions with an axe handle that has no head, for the Holy Spirit is the cutting edge.

A great deal of our Christian teaching makes little dent for eternity because we don't know what is the part of the divine Teacher and what is the part of the human teacher. We are fully cognizant of the fact that methods of themselves cannot draw men to Christ, yet methods of some kind are inherent in every process. If we aren't teaching by one method, we are teaching by another. There's no way to eliminate methods. The problem is to find God's ways of working, and work with Him, not to try to wheedle God into blessing our schemes. Since Christian teaching may be defined as discovering God's ways of working and working with Him, we need to learn by Scripture and by experience all God wants us to know of the ways of His Spirit. Not that we should try to unscrew the inscrutable, but those things which God has revealed belong to us and to our children (Deuteronomy 29:29).

As a teacher reads this final chapter of this book, it is suggested that he live for several days or weeks in John 14, 15, 16, where Christ Jesus told us so much about the Holy Spirit whom He would send to His people. Modern versions of the gospels often give us a more accurate translation for the word *Paraclete* than the word *Comforter* of the King James version. The term *Comforter* is much narrower

I CORINTHIANS 2:1—4:7

Our Part	God's Part
we come not with brilliance of speech or intellect	
we concentrate on Christ and His cross	
we rely not upon persuasion by words of human wisdom, but upon	the demonstration of the power of the Spirit that has been revealed by God
yet for mature believers we do speak spiritual wisdom	the Spirit unveils things never seen, heard that never occurred to natural man
	He shares even the deepest truths of God
	only He understands the thoughts of God
	He gives insight into God's grace
we set forth these spiritual truths in words	that the Spirit teaches
we appreciate them	by spiritual insight
we have the very thoughts of Christ	
we are mere servants	to whom the Lord has given a task
some of us plant, some water	but God gives the growth
we are nothing in ourselves, nothing compared with	God who gives the growth
the planter and waterer are one in aim	yet each gets his own reward according to his work
we are God's fellow workers; you are His field, His house	according to God's commission

one is the architect who lays the foundation, Christ, while
    another builds upon it
each one must be careful how he builds

we are God's holy temple
the world's wisdom is folly with God; we cannot boast of men
but everything (spiritual) belongs to you in Christ, in God
we are servants of Christ and trustees or stewards of God's
    truths, who must prove worthy of the trust

the judgment day will test by fire the character of
    each man's work
if his work stands the test, he will receive his reward
where the Spirit has His permanent home

our only true judge is God Himself
    who will expose secret motives
    and give praise accordingly
all we have is a gift from God,
    which excludes boasting

"Therefore, my beloved brethren, be ye stedfast, unmoveable, always abounding in the work of the
Lord, forasmuch as ye know that your labour is not in vain in the Lord" (1 Corinthians 15:58)

than the original idea of "One called alongside to help."
When we're in trouble we need comfort, but at all times we
need an indwelling Person to offset our ignorance and
infirmity and to intercede for us. Charles Williams, J. B.
Phillips, and James Moffatt use the general term *Helper* to
translate *Paraclete,* while Kenneth Wuest and the Revised
Standard Version employ the very suggestive word *Counselor.*

The following are the definite statements that John 14—
16 make about the Spirit:

> The Counselor, the Spirit of truth, the Holy Spirit
>   whom Christ will send from the Father
>   whom you know, for He dwells with you, and shall be in
>   you to be with you for ever
>
>   will bear witness to Christ
>   will bring to remembrance all that Christ has said to you
>   will glorify Christ
>
>   will teach you all things
>   will guide you into all the truth
>   will take what is Christ's and declare it to you
>   will declare to you the things that are to come
>
>   will convince the world of sin
>   of righteousness
>   of judgment.

With the divine enabling of the Holy Spirit, God's people
should assume their elevated relationship to Him as friend
rather than as servant or slave. Christ said to His disciples,
"No longer do I call you servants, for the servant does not
know what his master is doing; but I have called you
friends, for all that I have heard from my Father I have
made known to you" (John 15:14,15 RSV). Servants expect
to obey their master from a sense of duty, often blindly,
whereas friends are taken into confidence, friends cooper-

ate intelligently with the Master's aims and methods, from the motive of love that Christ stresses.

Not that we can expect to understand everything. But just as in His Word He has given us the momentous message of salvation, so He has given much in the way of method if we seek it. Even when we try to work intelligently with Him, there will be much that we can never understand because His ways are so much higher than our ways because He is God. Sometimes we can't even comprehend His purpose, yet it must be His, not ours. Our great concern is always the maintaining of our relationship with Him; our concentration must not be on our work. And our relationship with Him is constantly being assailed. When we can't understand His higher ways, we can only rest in our intimate union with Him. He Himself must give the security we need. If we haven't that, we will break down.

The Lord takes the initiative in choosing and appointing His disciples, but they are to go and bear fruit that will abide, because the Father gives them what they ask for. We note throughout the statements on discipleship the inextricable interweaving of the human and divine elements.

In 1 Corinthians 2:1—4:7 (*see* chart on pages 240, 241) we see the same delicate balance in the ministry of the Apostle Paul.

THE HOLY SPIRIT IN THE TEACHER HIMSELF

1. *The Holy Spirit seeks to become our life, deeper than thought or feeling.*

May we never cease to marvel that the Lord God Almighty, infinite and eternal, deigns to take up His abode in these frail, sinful bodies of ours! That He who created this vast universe of planets and suns and stars is concerned about the microcosm as well as the macrocosm, about the individual as well as the church, the body of Christ. That He seeks to give us fulness of life, the abundant life, eternal life here and now if only we allow Him to permeate every cell of our being with His glorious health and energy. Who would not prefer a radiant, glowing, enthusiastic person to a distressed, limping, weary one, and yet how many of us know from daily experience the exhilaration of the fulness of the Spirit? How many of us have been freed from our greatest enemy, our own warped and twisted selves?

Of course our contaminated human hearts are no fit temple for the Holy Spirit of God. It is Christ within us now who receives the Spirit just as it was He who received the Spirit when the third Person of the Trinity descended upon Him in a form like that of a dove at His baptism. It is only when we are united to Christ that we are ready to receive the Spirit, for He is the Spirit of Christ.

God's chief way of working in our day is to accept control of the inside of a man and to live His life for him. In the inmost core of our being He seeks to set up His throne and to reign supreme, to take control of man's will and work it for him. Deeper than consciousness, the Spirit works in every abyss of our personality. The depths of our beings are important, but the answer is not Freudianism, it is our divine Counselor, who alone probes our motives and desires. From the very center He then works out the miracle of Redemption in every aspect of our lives. He sanctifies us wholly, and prays in us with pleadings that cannot be uttered.

Andrew Murray in his classic work, *The Spirit of Christ*, points out again and again that the Spirit and the words of Christ are meant not only for the understanding, but for the whole life. Because we think of Christ's Spirit and Christ's words in relation to teaching, we naturally connect them with mental thoughts. They are meant for the life, deeper than thought or feeling, he keeps saying:

We want the Spirit to suggest to us certain conceptions of how Jesus will be with us and in us. And this is not what He does. The

Spirit does not dwell in the mind, but in the life. Not in what *we know,* but in what *we are* does the Spirit begin His work. Do not let us seek or expect at once a clear apprehension, a new insight, into this or any Divine truth. Knowledge, thought, feeling, action, all this is a part of that external religion which the external presence of Jesus had also wrought in the disciples. The Spirit was now to come, and, deeper down than all these, He was to be the Hidden Presence of Jesus within the depths of their personality. The Divine Life was in a newness of power to become their life. And the teaching of the Spirit would begin, not in word or thought, but in Power.[22]

2. *The Spirit works through the written Word to exalt the living Christ of the cross.*
　Again Andrew Murray says:

His words are Spirit and Life; they are not meant for the understanding (in the sense of the understanding alone), but for the Life. Coming in the Power of the Unseen Spirit, higher and deeper than all thought, they enter into the very roots of the Life, they have themselves a Divine Life, working out effectually with a Divine energy the Truth they express into the experience of those who receive them. As a consequence of this their spiritual character—this is the other lesson He wished His disciples to learn—these words of His need a spiritual nature to receive them. Seed needs a congenial soil: there must be life in the soil as well as in the seed. Not into the mind only, nor into the feelings, nor even into the will alone must the word be taken, but through them into the life. The centre of that life is man's spiritual nature, with conscience as its voice; there the authority of the word must be acknowledged. But even this is not enough: conscience dwells in man as a captive amid powers it cannot control. It is the Spirit that comes from God, the Spirit that Christ came to bring, becoming our life, receiving the word and assimilating it into our life, that will make them to become the Truth and Power in us.[23]

The Spirit uses the written revelation to show people spiritual Reality, which is the Lamb of God slain before the foundation of the world to take away the sin of the world. When the Spirit illumines the sacred page, it becomes more than words and sentences on a sheet of paper—it becomes the very voice of God to the individual heart. Christ becomes more than a good man, a good example, a historical figure—He becomes the very Son of God wooing the sinner to Himself, a real Person seated at the right hand of God in the heavens, but working also in this world. Then the human creature falls at His feet, acknowledging His right and His alone to save, to rule, to judge the world.

3. *The only work that counts is His work through us.*

How much so-called Christian service is mere sterile busyness in the energy of the flesh! No doubt most agencies and organizations were originally set up to meet real needs. The initial push to get them going probably required more than human effort. But as routines and patterns become established, the organizations continue to move only because they have smooth grooves and ruts to run in. As meeting succeeds meeting and week succeeds week, the motions are performed perfunctorily but the burden and the urgency are lost. The original flame subsides to a glow and then dies out. When the energy of the Spirit vanishes, the workers may as well begin again, on their knees.

Paul said, ". . . I laboured more abundantly than they all: yet not I, but the grace of God which was with me" (1 Corinthians 15:10). And "Whereunto I also labour, striving according to his working, which worketh in me mightily" (Colossians 1:29). It is our talent that the Spirit uses, our insights, our enthusiasm, our hands—but it is His use of them that makes all the difference between wasted blight and jumbo harvest. He could easily work directly with souls, could set them to seeking and finding their Savior. Sometimes He does. But usually He condescends to limit Himself to what He can do in cooperation with us.

Suppose Billy Graham had said in his youth, "Some day

I'd like to go all out for God, but first I'd like to gratify a
few of my own desires. First I'd like to have a few adventures in foreign travel and get acquainted with a few interesting people." How would the adventures of his own
making have compared with the adventures that God had
in store for him?

For all of us God has amazing worlds to conquer, with
great excitement along the way, in addition to suffering, if
only we aren't satisfied with our own paltry plans that we
can envisage for ourselves. He seeks for us nothing less
than the power of His resurrection and the fellowship of
His sufferings. He says, ". . . work out your own salvation
with fear and trembling. For it is God which worketh in you
both to will and to do of his good pleasure" (Philippians
2:12,13).

4. *Our part is to be ready to receive the divine guidance and power
that the Spirit comes to give.*

Just to be ready to receive! Who shouldn't be ready to
receive? Yet many of us aren't because we are full of ourselves. There isn't room for Him. We are so full of our own
plans and purposes and activities that we have no time left
for waiting upon the Lord. We must wait upon Him in
order to receive from Him. We cannot dash into His presence to pick up a directive on our way to a meeting. We
cannot flip on the power switch when spiritual illumination
grows dim.

When we think we're waiting for God, He is usually waiting for us, waiting for us to get ready to receive what we
need. We're inclined to rely upon our own resources until
He brings us to a crisis where we can't. Only when we get
really desperate, when we experience our own helplessness, are we ready to wait upon Him. Our essential need is
for the Lord Himself, nothing less. We receive of Him by
thirsting for Him with our whole being, by coming to Him
in deep communion, by drinking of Him until we are filled

(Luke 11:13). When we see how truly dry and parched we are in ourselves, we thirst and come and drink until He can infuse His own life into ours. When we reach the saturation point we're bursting to share Him with others. We then have Reality to share.

"In the Old Testament," says Andrew Murray, "it was man's best with God's help. Now God is offering to undertake the whole responsibility. He doesn't blame us for what we don't do, but for what we don't let Him do for us." There is no other explanation for men who have been mightily used of God. An outline of their sermons or teaching plans may be similar to those of others who are getting meager results. Said Billy Graham: "If God should take His hands off my life, my lips would turn to clay. I'm no great intellectual, and there are thousands of men who are better preachers than I am. You can't explain me if you leave out the supernatural. I am but a tool of God."

5. *We must practice active submission to the Holy Spirit, and be passive toward the strivings of the self-life.*

Only a tool, only a channel are we in the hands of God. Yes, in one sense; yet both these figures are inadequate because tools and channels are dead and mechanical while human instruments have wills of their own. The Lord does not purpose to deaden our wills or render them mechanical, but to activate them under His control. He does not propose to break our wills, for we shall need the full force of them in our struggle against evil. He wants us deliberately to identify our wills with His.

This will mean the total submission of the old self-life with its longings and strivings. This means that we shall be constantly looking to Him rather than around us, constantly listening to Him when it is more natural to talk, constantly obeying His slightest indication without question. "Behold, as the eyes of servants look unto the hand of their masters, and as the eyes of a maiden unto the hand of her mistress; so our eyes wait upon the Lord our

God . . ." (Psalms 123:2). Are we fresh for any opportunity as we trust Him implicitly to pour His own creative life continually through us?

THE HOLY SPIRIT IN THE PROCESS OF TEACHING

1. *We must keep the person of Christ central rather than the work.*

"The greatest competitor of devotion to Jesus is service for Him." How often we start a project in utter love for Him, with the purest of motives. But as the process becomes complicated and personalities grate upon each other, persons tend unconsciously to protect their egos and defend their own rights. With the result that Christ is pushed off center by the pressure of the work itself. When the Spirit of God is grieved because Christ deserves pre-eminence in all things, the work drags and people grow discouraged.

If Christ is truly real to us, everything else is less real. If we abide in Him as the branch abides in the vine, fruit is the natural consequence. In order to bear more fruit upward, our roots have to go deeper down in the Lord. More than servants to work for Him, the Lord seeks sons to fellowship with Him. Concentration on the work produces barrenness. Our chief work is to reflect Christ. The Spirit jealously guards the centrality of Christ unless His ministry is quenched.

2. *Insight that is both spiritual and educational enables the leader to penetrate deeply into personality.*

We saw from our study of the gospels that Christ was able to reach the inner recesses of men with eternal truth because He knew man generically and He knew men individually. On the basis of this knowledge, He beamed the truth specifically to the inner need of each man. How can Christ teach through us when we are not able to plumb the depths of other human beings? The Holy Spirit is the answer. He knows what our pupils are thinking and feeling at the moment, their private desires and ambitions.

When we pray in the Spirit that Christ will be formed in our pupils, the Spirit prays according to the will of God with discernment that is divine, and yet He is praying in us. Therefore the prayer will be answered through us. In that case it often happens that after a sermon or lesson a person will say to a Christian leader, "How did you know this or that about me? Who told you?" The Christian leader will probably answer, "I didn't know that definitely about you, but the Spirit of God did, and I seek to work in the Spirit."

Not that the leading of the Spirit precludes study and preparation on our part. We are to do what we can in the Spirit. We are to study our pupils as diligently as possible, for the Spirit does not give us what we can get for ourselves. Nor does He, the Spirit of love and power and discipline, work with lazy Christians. But together we may possess the insight into human personality that we need.

We find an example of this extraordinary insight in Acts 8:9–24. After Simon the magician saw the remarkable demonstrations of power that were performed by the Holy Spirit, he offered the apostles money if they would give him that power. "How dare you think you could buy the gift of God!" Peter sternly rebuked him. "You can have no share in this ministry for your heart is not honest before God. I can see inside you, that you are bitter with jealousy, bound with your own sin."

3. *It is the peculiar ministry of the Holy Spirit to make the outer Word an inner experience.*

No other teacher can be both an outer and an inner factor. No other teacher can get inside the pupil to perform a personal, intimate operation in the depths of his being. As God's active agent or method, the Spirit does subjectively within the pupil all that Christ has done objectively without. Educational method is simply finding out how the Spirit works and working with Him rather than against Him, as we so often do even with the best of intentions. As the human teacher works with the divine Teacher, the Scriptural record becomes more than letters and sounds and words; it becomes the living voice of God speaking to the heart.

As the human teacher in the power of the Spirit seeks the avenue of approach that will give the Word entrance into the city of mansoul (the inner citadel of the life), the Spirit serves as the traffic officer to clear the road so that the Word may have free access. As the royal entourage approaches, mansoul beholds the King Himself and bows before Him in reverent homage. So enamored is mansoul with the nobility of the King that he invites both the King and His court to live permanently in his city. The Sovereign, who was formerly known only by hearsay, is now given the rule of the city. This new rule begins immediately to transform the life of the city.

Without making Himself conspicuous, the third member of the Trinity acts as Expediter to remove obstructions so that both written and Living Word may have free course in the life. The human teacher is merely a humble apprentice for the divine Executive, an understudy who likewise seeks to get the pupil interacting with the Word.

Acts 10:44 records the fact that as Peter preached the Word in the house of Cornelius, the Holy Spirit fell on all who were listening. Conversely, Stephen upbraided the Jews, "You obstinate people, heathen in your thinking, heathen in the way you are listening to me now! It is always the same—you never fail to resist the Holy Spirit!" (Acts 7:51 PHILLIPS).

4. *All problems are rooted in the spiritual, yet they also need solution on the human level.*

While the church at Antioch was worshiping the Lord and fasting, the Holy Spirit said to them, ". . . Set apart for me Barnabas and Saul for the work to which I have called them" (Acts 13:2 RSV). This call involved questions as to where they should go, whether these two men should go together or separately, whether anyone else should go with them. After the first leg of their journey, they separated, Barnabas taking with him Mark, and Paul taking Silas (Acts 15:39,40). Having been forbidden by the Spirit to speak the Word in Asia, they went through Phrygia and Galatia. When they attempted to go into Bithynia, the Spirit prevented them, so they went down to Troas. There Paul had a vision of a man of Macedonia who was beseeching them to come over to his country to help (Acts 16:6–9).

"The missionary journeys of Paul exhibit an extraordinary combination of strategic planning and keen sensitiveness to the guidance of the Spirit of God."[24]

Even after our pupils today discover the principles of God's Word, they are often at a loss to know how to implement them in their own lives in today's world. The situations today may seem so different from those of Bible times that they see no carry-over. Some of them are earnestly seeking the will of the Lord, but they don't know what His will is. In order to choose among the possible alternatives, they need the express leading of the Spirit, just as Saul and Barnabas were led away from Asia and Bithynia to Macedonia. They may need guidance in thinking through what steps *they* would need to take in order to go to the mission field. Until they have visualized what would be involved in obeying the Lord's command to go, and how they would receive spiritual supplies, they might not be ready to make the decision.

5. *Although we make thorough lesson preparation in the Spirit ahead of time, we should also be ready for the Spirit's leading during the lesson.*

Of course the Spirit leads us ahead of time just as clearly as during a lesson, yet we cannot envisage ahead of time all the situations that will arise. If Christ is truly teaching in His own way through us, He will make full use of the spontaneous questions and comments and needs that come up in a participative group where people are interacting with the Word of God. If the Word of God is doing the work of God, things are going to happen, and we want to be ready to guide the group as fast as they are ready to go. We need the liberty of the Spirit to incorporate these ideas into the ongoing process.

Often it is in the midst of a dynamic situation that teachers and pupils get their best ideas. In the midst of stimulating research new relationships are seen and new purposes developed. It is exciting to have pupils declare, "We ought to be doing more to maintain the unity of the Spirit in the bond of peace. Why don't we send a committee to the trustees to discuss our part of the budget instead of criticizing them?" Problems that seem insoluble when individuals ponder them alone are viewed in a much more optimistic light when the Spirit of God is free to move a group in the direction of God's will.

The interaction that Christ achieved in His teaching was the result of His union and identity with the Father. His ability to start anywhere the pupil happened to be and to use any comment to lead step by step to eternal truth and on into action was the result of His embodiment of the truth. He was free to use any aspect of eternal truth at any time and to reflect it in His own person at every moment. As we teachers apply ourselves diligently to the Word and to prayer, the Spirit will give us, too, supernatural wisdom and power to make use of every opportunity. As we are borne along by the Spirit, the design of the lesson grows richer and deeper than the one we had originally prepared, though our previous preparation has figured largely as the basis for what actually happens.

How superlative ought to be any form of Christian teaching, with so many supernatural distinctives—the infallible written Word revealing our Creator-Redeemer God who sent His Son to be King of kings, and the Holy Spirit working within the teacher, upon or within the pupil, to exalt the Savior through the inscripturated record! If we teachers begin to enter into our heritage in Christ, to appropriate and reflect the Lord our life, we should continually be seeing the results that Christ saw—people believing, witnessing, following, and obeying. What a crime for any session to be dull when it ought to be positively exciting, prosaic when it ought to be dynamic, boring when it ought to be a great adventure!

The infinite resources of heaven are at our disposal, waiting for us to be ready to receive fulness of life and power to teach. Think of the loss if we fail our generation, fail to transmit the gospel in its full force, fail to demonstrate the superiority of Christian teaching over secular teaching. A revolutionary gospel in a revolutionary age calls for revolutionary teaching that revolutionizes lives. The solution to today's problems is not more glamorous entertainments in the church, more trick gadgets, more contests with more expensive prizes, but more Christian leaders in whom Christ can work in His own way in the power of the Spirit.

If anyone would be a true Christian teacher,
   let him deny his own prejudices
   and take up Christ's methods, though they're not the easy
     ones,
   and follow the Master Teacher.
For whosoever would save himself
   shall lose the real thrill of teaching;
   and whosoever shall give himself wholly to teaching in the distinctive Christian way shall reap eternal results.
For what doth it profit a teacher to give out the whole truth
   if he loses his pupil?
But the Savior will reveal Himself by the Spirit
   when He is again allowed to teach in His own way through the
     teacher.   (After Mark 8:34–36)

NOTES

1. Daniel L. Marsh, "The Place of Religion in Education," *Personal Growth Leaflet* 150 (Washington: National Education Assoc.), pp. 14–16. Reprinted by permission.

2. A. W. Tozer, *The Pursuit of God* (Harrisburg, Pa.: Christian Publications Inc., 1948), p. 8. Reprinted by permission of the publishers.

3. *Ibid.*, pp. 9, 10.

4. "Are You a Firsthander?" *Christian Life*, April, 1954, p. 27.

5. "Keswick," *Eternity*, September, 1954, p. 10.

6. "Advice to Evangelicals," *United Evangelical Action*, February 15, 1950, p. 9.

7. F. Bettex, *The Bible the Word of God* (Cincinnati: Jennings and Graham, 1904), pp. 52–54.

8. Merrill C. Tenney, *The Genius of the Gospels* (Grand Rapids: William B. Eerdmans Publishing Co., 1951), p. 116.

9. Kenneth Wuest, *Philippians in the Greek New Testament* (Grand Rapids: William B. Eerdmans Publishing Co., 1953), pp. 35, 36.

10. Frank E. Gaebelein, *The Pattern of God's Truth* (New York: Oxford University Press, 1954), p. 35.

11. Andrew Murray, *The Spirit of Christ* (London: Nisbet and Co., 1888), p. 228.

12. *Ibid.*, p. 266.

13. *Ibid.*, p. 87.

14. Kathryn Blackburn Peck, "Jottings," *Church School Builder*, March, 1953, p. 11.

15. Matilda F. Etecht, *Christian Index*, quoted in *Moody Monthly*, October, 1929, p. 80.

16. V. Raymond Edman, *Storms and Starlight* (Wheaton, Ill.: Van Kempen Press, 1953), p. 10.

17. J. R. Gibb, Grace N. Platts, Lorraine F. Miller, *Dynamics of Participative Groups* (St. Louis: John S. Swift Co., 1951), p. 65. Reprinted by permission.

18. A. W. Tozer, "We Need Sanctified Thinkers," *The Alliance Weekly*, November 9, 1955, p. 2.

19. Oswald Chambers, *My Utmost for His Highest* (New York: Dodd, Mead and Co., 1935), p. 307.

20. *Ibid.,* p. 352.

21. Raymond Calkins, *How Jesus Dealt with Men* (New York: Abingdon-Cokesbury Press, 1942), p. 206.

22. Murray, *op. cit.,* pp. 101, 102.

23. *Ibid.,* p. 44.

24. F.F. Bruce, *Commentary on the Book of the Acts* (Grand Rapids: William B. Eerdmans Publishing Co., 1954), p. 325.